How to Make $1M in a Few Years by Stock Investment
Fundamentals and Applications in Bull and Bear Markets

2019 Edition
Printed in black/white

Shoichiro Nakamura

Copyright©S.Nakamura 2019
Alll rights reserved

ISBN: 9781792938078

First Publication January 2019

The author will take no responsibilities on any loss of the readers.

About the author

The author is a scientist but not a professional trader in stock market. The reader might ask why such a person would write a book on stock investment. Here is the answer. In any scientific research, a huge amount of data is analyzed whether the subject is theoretical or experimental. In the stock market research, a large amount of data is analyzed also to find out the best way to grow money. So there is a significant similarity between the two, and author's experience and knowledge in scientific research turned out to be very usefull. Also stock investment research needs some mathematics knowledge. The author has profound knowledge and skill there.

Another reason that is more important is that the author developed his own method of stock investment that is highly lucrative and easy to apply even for the beginners in stock investing. This book describes the fundamentals of the author's method, and their practical applications. So who is better qualified than this author to write his own method?

The author has published more than ten books on other subjects including mathematics, which may be found at amazon.com using his full name as search key words.

Contents

Preface 1

1 Math Analysis of Hypothetical Scenarios 3

2 Buying Long and Selling Short 4

3 Stock Price Oscillations 5

4 Bull ETF and Bear EFT 6

5 Charts and Price Indicators 10

    5.1 Candlestick Symbols 10

    5.2 Wicks of Candles 13

    5.3 MA, SMA, EMA 15

    5.4 RSI 22

    5.5 Method of Computing RSI 25

    5.6 MACD 27

    5.7 Calculation of MACD 29

    5.8 Divergence of MACD 31

    5.9 FastSTO Indicator 35

    5.10 SlowSTO Indicator 36

    5.11 What the Indicators Do Not Do Well 40

    5.12 Is the Market in Up Trend or Down Trend 45

    5.13 Advanced/Decline Line Indicator 46

    5.14 How to identify the Day of Peak and Day of Bottom 49

6 Long Term and Short Term Investment in Stocks and ETFs 55

    6.1 High-grade Stocks and Long Term Investment 556

    6.2 Technology ETFs 61

    6.3 Crude Oil, Natural GAS and Energy 64

    6.4 Foreign Investment Funds 68

- 6.5 Volatility Index Funds and SP 500 Bull/ Bear 3x Funds 76
- 6.6 Penny Stocks and Marijuana Stocks 81
- 6.7 Bitcoin 83
- 6.8 Gold and Silver 86

7 Relations between DOWJ and Stocks/ETFs 99
- 7.1 Substantial Losses in Downturn of Stock Market 99
- 7.2 Early Detection of a Downturn 103
- 7.3 Making Money in Volatile Falling Market 110
- 7.4 Opportunities after a Bottom of DOWJ 111
- 7.5 How DOWJ and Gold/Gold stocks are related 115

8 Review of Stocks and Funds 116

9 Rules of What To Do Now 161

Preface

The most fundamental principle of investing in the stock market is simple and clear. That is to buy when stocks or funds are cheap, ideally at a bottom price, and sell them when the price becomes high, ideally at a peak price. However, practicing this simple principle is not always easy because there are so many choices of stocks and funds (i.e. ETFs and ETNs)[1] in addition to that there are so many data to look at to make decisions.

The author developed a method to make selection of funds as well as to find the best timing of buy and sell. This method is not only simple but also helps make awesome gains from stock trading. This book describes in details the author's method. The contents of this book do not include anything unnatural or eccentric. Everything is common sense, yet the essence of this book has never been published in an organized way. The fundamentals written in this book, however, will have an extraordinary impact on the way you invest in the stock market.

The method of investing in stock market written in this book uses a few stock price indicators as important tools. Although all indicators are derived mathematically, the readers are not forced to read the mathematical discussions. However, the reader should learn how the indicators are related to the movements of stock prices, because we need to use the stock indicators when making decisions of the timings to buy and sell.

A frequent question asked is how much money is necessary to start stock investment using the methods of this book. The answer is that $1,000 is enough, but $10,000 is better.

We do not need to set a goal on how fast the initial investment will grow. However, you might become aware that, with the method described in this book, the initial investment may grow to 100 times in four years.

If you are still young, you do not need to make money so fast. By the method of this book, however, your wealth will accumulate, so eventually your investment will reach a huge sum. Important is the fundamentals explained in this book.

---

[1] The meaning of ETF, ETN and fund will be explained in Chapter 4

Before starting your reading, open stockcharts.com that includes graphs of stock prices plus stock price indicators, RSI, MACD, SlowSTO, all of which will be explained in details as you read this book.

Normally stock investors dislike downturn of the stock market. Contrarily in this book, we take downturns of stock markets as opportunities. In fact, with some knowledge about stock and funds, much money can be earned in bearish stock markets. This book writes how to gain in both bull and bear markets.

Stocks can be traded either as individual stocks or a bundle of stocks. A bundle is called a fund. Funds include mutual funds, ETFs and ETNs. A fund can be 1x, 2x or 3x bull fund, or 1x, 2x or 3x bear fund. Here, 1x is a straight bundle of stock shares, 2x is a bundle of two times of stock shares compared to 1x, and 3x is a bundle of 3 times. The 2x or 3x is equivalent to buying 2 or 3 times, respectively, of stock shares using the power of margin. We aim to buy and sell with a high yield. As such, 2x and 3x funds best satisfy our objectives rather than individual stocks and 1x funds. The prices of bull 2x and 3x funds go up when the market is ascending, and the prices of bear 2x and 3x funds go up when the market is descending.

In this book we explain both stocks and funds, but in the actual investment, we will buy and sell 2x and 3x funds most of times.

The figures illustrated in the book will soon be outdated. The readers are encouraged to open stockcharts.com and obtain most updated price chart for the stock or funds of the investor's interest. However, having old charts is not necessarily a bad thing. Obtaining detailed stock price charts of the past becomes difficult if time is past more than 6 months. Therefore, the price charts in this book may become valuable as archive. History is important in learning. Another advantage of having old charts is that the readers can train the reader's ability of guessing what came after a selected date on the figure while masking the charts after the date, and checking accuracy of the guess by removing the mask.

Finally the author would like to thank Dan Brilhart and Chikako Migishima for their assistance in proofreading the manuscript of this book.

1 Math Analysis of Hypothetical Scenarios

Suppose the initial investment is $1000, and our goal is to increase it to $1M in 10 years, or equivalently 1000-fold in 10 years. Then, what is the necessary annual rate of increase?

To answer this question we need to solve the equation:
$$X^{10} = 1000$$
where X is the rate of increase in one year. The solution is
$$X = (1000)^{(1/10)} = 1.995$$
or approximately 2. In other words, if the investment doubles each year, the initial investment of $1000 increases to $1M in 10 years. To get the annual rate of 2, what shall be an average rate of gain per month? The answer of this question is obtained by solving
$$Z^{12} = 2$$
or equivalently $\log(Z) = \log(2)/12 = 0.0251$, where the base of log is 10. The answer is $Z = 10^{0.0251} = 1.059$, which is equivalent to about 6% increase per month.

If the methods of this book are applied successfully, an average gain of 6% per month will not be difficult because chances of obtaining 20% to 30% gain per month can happen often.

If the annual rate of 2 is too hard, how about reducing it to 1.5, which is much easier to achieve? If your investment increases to 1.5-fold in one year, then an initial investment of $1000 needs about 17 years to reach $1M. Still this gain is achieved only by a very small fraction of investors in the stock market. If you are young and add fresh money of $1000 to your account every year, the number of years to reach $1M is much shorter.

As another thought experiment, how long does it take for the initial investment of $1000 to reach $1M, if the annual rate is 3? By writing the number of years as Y, we need to solve the equation:
$$3^Y = 1000$$

The answer is Y=6.28, or roughly 6 years. With an annual rate of 3, an initial investment of $10,000 reaches $1M in 4.4 years. To reach the annual rate of 3, the monthly rate should be about 10%, which is only 4% higher than the monthly rate for the annual rate of 2, and may even achievable.

2 Buying Long and Selling Short

The most basic trading of stocks and funds is to buy stock or fund shares and sell when its price gets higher. In more professional terms, this buying action is called "buying long".

On the other hand, stock or ETF shares may be sold even when the shares are not owned by the seller. This action is called "selling short", which is profitable if the stock or ETF price goes down. To sell short, the investor borrows shares from the stock broker and sells. The investor pays some fee for borrowing shares from the broker. The stock shares sold short must be returned to the broker by buying back at some point in the future. The broker may not always have the shares to be borrowed, so short selling is not always possible. Availability of the stock shares to lend depends on time and popularity of the stock.

Short selling is very easy on an online stock broker site. As soon as you attempt to trade a stock, your are given choices among, "buy", "sell", "short sell". To short sell, you only need to click on "short sell" and fill in the box for the number of shares. If the broker has shares to lend to you, your action will go through. Sometimes the broker does not have the shares you wish to sell short, however. When the stock price descends, many investors try to sell short, so the stock shares available to borrow become scarce. In general, the larger the market of the stock or fund, the easier to borrow.

Investors should become familiar and experienced with short selling. With capability of both buying long and selling short, opportunities of making money in stock market significantly increases.

In applying the methods of this book, however, chance of trading individual stock is small, because the leveraged funds (2x and 3x ETF and ETN) are more powerful than individual stocks. Many of them have a bear counterpart. So short selling may be used only if the fund has no bear counterpart. When the fund does not have its bear counterpart, you can sell short the bull fund.

3 Stock Price Oscillations

The stock prices constantly move like ocean waves. They go up for some time, and then they go down in oscillation. Their oscillations are compound of long waves and short waves. The long waves are our friend, but short waves are often called "noise" which disturbs the investors.

Stock prices never go to zero unless the company which sells the stock is closed for bankruptcy or for some other special reasons.

Stock price of a company is affected by various factors of the company such as the total assets, expected profit, and demand for the stock, and the stock market conditions. The stock price goes higher if the number of people who want to buy it is greater than the number of people who want to sell it. Policies of government or even political announcements greatly influence the stock prices. For example, after the recent announcement of the US president regarding the import tax, the stock prices of many companies plummeted. Prices of some stocks are sensitive to the government reports of the consumer price index and employment rate.

Another factor that affects the stock prices is the index of US dollars. It is well known that when the value of US dollars ascends, exporting from US becomes more difficult so the stock prices go down. Recently a notable incidence occurred in the middle of June 2018. A sudden surge of US dollars followed by a European Central Bank's policy decision pushed dollars further. The gold speculators started short selling of gold in the gold futures market. The short selling of the gold futures snowballed toward August of 2018, and all of gold price and sock prices of gold miners plunged in an extreme magnitude. Silver and silver miners prices descended as gold price.

The 1st principle of stock trading is simply to buy when the stocks or funds (ETF/ETN) are oversold and sell when overbought. The 2nd principle is to sell short when the stocks are overbought (and high). Buying bear funds has the same effects as selling bull funds short.

In the real operation, the decisions of buy/sell have to be made without exactly knowing the price movements in the future. To make such decisions, the stock price indicators such as RSI, MACD and SlowSTO will be very important tools.

Although the price indicators are important, the most important information for timing buy and sell comes from the shape of candles at the price peaks and bottoms and changes of the candles from the previous day. The candles and the price indicators will be explained in details in Chapter 5.

4 Bull ETF and Bear EFT

ETF is an abbreviation of Exchange Traded Fund, which is a bundle of many stocks just like mutual funds. However, the difference from mutual funds is that the price is determined for each trade just like stocks but unlike mutual funds. There is another type of funds called Index Funds[2], but we will not touch on them in this book.

An ETF many be 1x, 2x and 3x. It means that the price movements of 1x ETF is proportional to the average price of the stocks included in the ETF, the price movements of 2x ETF is twice as high as 1x ETF, and the 3x ETF 3 times. The 2x and 3X ETF use the margin trades automatically. Therefore, the profits of 2x and 3x ETF are double or tripled respectively compared to 1x ETF. Of course in case of a loss, the total loss is doubled or tripled, respectively.

---

[2] Read "Differences between ETF and index fund" at
https://www.wallstreetmojo.com/etf-vs-index-funds/

An ETF is either a bull ETF or a bear ETF. The price of a bull ETF goes up as the average price of the involved stocks goes up. On the other hand, a bear ETF goes down inversely. Buying a bear ETF is essentially the same as short selling of the bull ETF. A bear ETF can be 1x, 2x or 3x too. The 2x and 3x ETF are usually not suitable to long term investment. The reason is that the costs of maintaining 2x and 3x ETFs are higher than the 1x ETFs. The prices of 2x and 3x ETFs go down in a long term even if the prices of the stocks do not change at all, because the price of an ETF includes the cost of maintenance. However, if the rate of the price increase of a 2x ETF or 3x ETF is higher than the cost, it can be used as a long term investment.

ETN (Exchange Traded Note) is also a bundle of stocks similarly to ETF, but the difference from ETF is in its operation and fee included in the price. From the investor's point of view, its difference is negligibly small, particularly when trading is in short term. We may call both ETF and ETN as "fund".

Table 4.1 shows major ETFs and ETNs. The ETNs included in the table are USLV／DSLV and UWT／DWT

Table 4.1 Major bull and bear funds

Bull	Bear	Leverage	Contents
NUGT	DUST	3x	Gold miners
JNUG	JDST	3x	Junior gold miners
GDL		1x	Gold miners
GDX		1x	Gold miners
GDXJ		1x	Junior gold miners
USLV (ETN)	DSLV (ETN)	3x	Silver mines
FAS	FAZ	3x	Financial
BRZU		3x	Brazil
INDL		3x	India
YINN		3x	China
CHAU		2x	China
CHIX		1x	China
RUSL	RUSS	3x	Russia
MEXX		3x	Mexico
TECL	TECS	3x	Technology
SOXL	SOXS	3x	Semiconductor
UBOT		3x	Robotics, artificial intelligence
LABU	LABD	3x	Bio technology

GBTC (trust)		1x	Bitcoin
ERX	ERY	3x	Energy
GASL	GASX	3x	Natural gas
GUSH	DRIP	3x	Natural gas, oil
UCO	SCO	1x	Crude oil
UWT (ETN)	DWT (ETN)	3x	Crude oil
USOU	USOD	3x	Crude oil
TNA	TZA	3x	Small industries
SPXL	SPXS	3x	SP 500
	TVIX	2x	SP 500

For illustration, price charts of a pair of bull and bear funds are shown in Figures 4.1 and 4.2. By comparing the two figures, it can be seen that the price movements are opposite. That is, when the price of the bull changes 5% up, the bear ETF's price goes down about 5%. However, the two rates are not exactly same, but always there is some difference. The difference is considered to come from the differences in the demand/supply of the bull and bear ETFs and the cost of maintenance of each ETF.

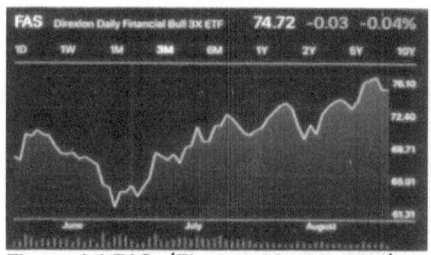 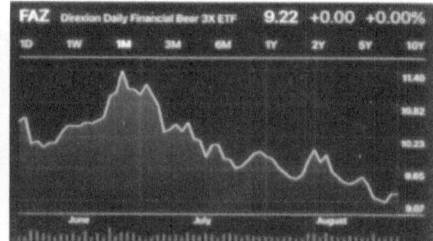

Figure 4.1 FAS (Financial bull 3x ETF)   Figure 4.2 FAS (Financial bear 3x ETF)

SOXL is one of the bull ETFs listed in Table 4.1. SOXS is the counterpart of SOXL and a bear 3xETF. Figure 4.3 shows the price movements of SOXL.

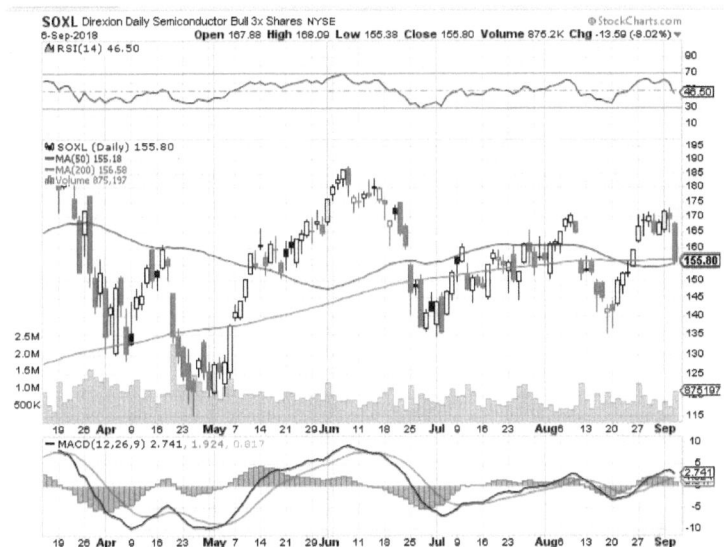

Figure 4.3   Price movement of SOXL

If SOXL is bought on 1 May 2018 at a price in the price bottom of $125/share, and sold later on 3 June 2018 at a price peak of $185, then the rate of profit is 185/125=1.48, or a gain of 48%.

Figure 4.4   Price movement of SOXS

Look at Figure 4.4. After SOXL is sold on 3 June 2018, suppose SOXS is bought immediately at $8.7/share using all the money available after selling SOXL, and sold on 1 July 2018 at $11.5/share. The rate of gain is 11.5/8.7=1.32, or 32% gain. The total rate of profit of SOXL and SOXS is (1.48)x(1.32) = 1.95, or 95% gain. Chances like this example visit us many times as we watch price charts of several 3x funds.

In conclusion, the reason why our methods of investment have such a high yield potential is in using both bull and bear 2x and 3x funds. If only individual stocks are traded, there is no chance to achieve this level of increasing the assets.

5 Charts and Price Indicators

The most important tools for stock trading are the stock/fund price charts and the stock/fund price indicators. In this section we explain how to read the stock/fund price charts and use stock/fund price indicators.

Although there are many stock price charts available on internet, we exclusively use stockcharts.com because it provides many stock price indicators. The only drawback of this site is that the length of history is limited to 2.5 years. In case price chart of a longer time is desired, use one of the following links:

> https://finance.yahoo.com/lookup/
> https://www.marketwatch.com/markets
> https://www.marketwatch.com/investing/fund/soxl
> https://www.investing.com/charts/stocks-charts

For a quick look at major market indices, the first sites above are useful. The last one is interactive, where long term charts are available.

5.1 Candlestick Symbols

Candlestick symbols are very often used in stock price charts. The candlestick symbols were originally developed in Japan, therefore, many words associated with the candlestick patterns are in Japanese language.

The two most fundamental patterns of the candlesticks are shown in Figures 5.1 and 5.2. A candle stick is used for the movements of a stock for a period, where the period is a day in most uses, but can be one hour, ten minutes, a week, or even month, depending on who produced that chart. The candle in Figure 5.1 called a bull candle has an empty box and two thin lines called wicks, one on the top and another at the bottom. The vertical direction along the candle is the direction of the price coordinate, the top of the box is the final price of the stock during the period, and the bottom of the box is the opening price. The top of the upper wick is the highest price during the period, while the bottom of the lower wick is the lowest during the period.

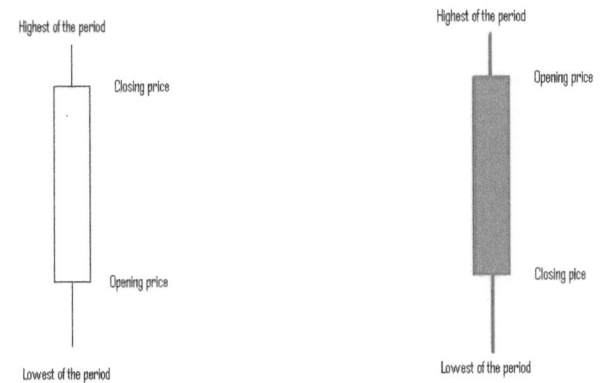

Figure 5.1 Candle in black   **Figure 5.2 Candle in red**

The candle of Figure 5.2 called a bear candle is normally printed in red color, while the top of the box is the opening price and the bottom of the box is the closing price. The top of the upper wick and the bottom of the lower wick have the same meaning as those in Figure 5.2.

The candle in Figure 5.3 has the same meaning as Figure 5.2, which is used when the closing price is higher than in the prior candlestick. The candle of Figure 5.4, where the border of the candle and wicks are in red color, has the same meaning as Figure 5.1, but used when the closing price is lower than that of the prior candle stick.

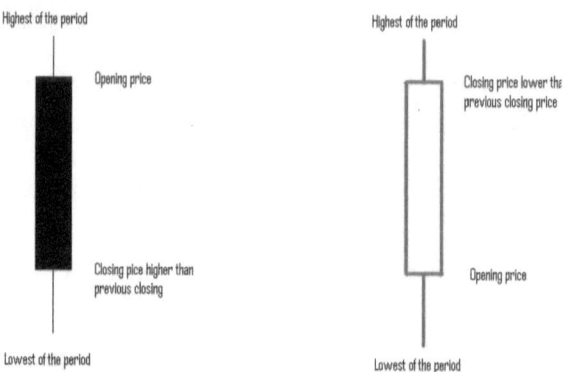

Figure 5.3 Candle in black   **Figure 5.4 Candle in red lines**

In some price charts, candles of Figure 5.3 and Figure 5.4 are not used.

Another type of symbols, shown in the figures below, called OHCL (open-high-low-close) bars are equivalent to candles.

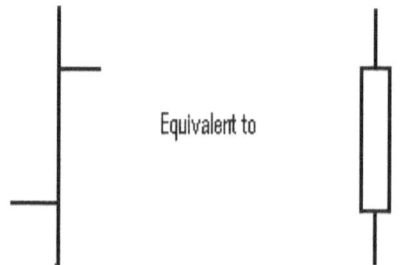

Figure 5.5 (Left in black, right in black lines)

Figure 5.6 (Left in black or red, right in red)

As stated earlier, it is important to check the definition of the period defined for a stock price chart because the definition of period may be different for each chart. A chart using OHCL bars is illustrated in Figure 5.7. OHCL bars can be used without color so they are used more often in black/white printing

Figure 5.7 Example of a price chart using OHCL bars

5.2 Wicks of Candles

Wicks of a candle often tell very important information.

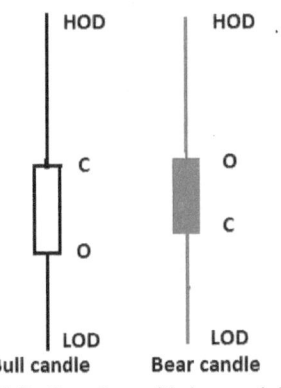

Figure 5.8 Candles with long wicks

In Figure 5.8, the left is a bull candle, same as Figure 5.1 except the wicks are longer. The opening price started at the level of O, and the closing price is at C. In between, however, the price came down to the level LOD (lowest of the day) and also went up to the level of HOD (highest of the day) before ending at C. It tells that, most likely, the price opened at O but came down to LOD and went up to HOD and came down to C to end the day. The long upper wick of this candle tells us that the price ascended to HOD but resisted to go higher and came back and ended at C. It means that a reversal of the ascending price happened during the day. If this is the peak day, the price of the next day is very likely lower.

Therefore, if a bull candle appears with a long upper wick after a serried of bull candles in the past, a peak is likely have arrived.

A bull candle on the left of Figure 5.8 with long lower wick may appear at the bottom of the price movement after a series of bear candles in the past. The long lower wick means that the price descended to LOD but resisted to go lower but rather ascended to the level of HOC and came down to C to end the day. It means that a reversal of the descending price happened at LOD. This is likely signals that the bottom has arrived.

A bear candle on the right of Figure 5.8 with a long upper wick may appear at a peak. In this case the price that opened at O ascended to HOD, but resisted to higher came down to EOD and ended at C. This signals that this day is likely the peak day, and the next day will be lower

A bear candle with a long lower wick may appear at a bottom. In this case the price that opened at O ascended to HOD, came down to EOD but resisted to do down further but ascended and ended at C. This signals that this day is likely the bottom day, and the next day will be higher.

Figure 5.9 includes examples of candles with long upper wicks at peaks and candles with long lower wicks

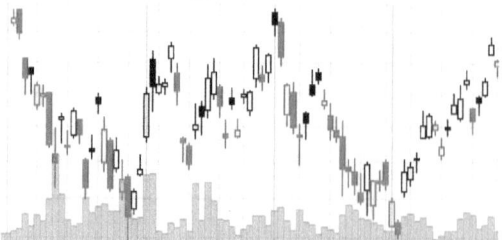

Figure 5.9 Example of candles

Identification of bottoms and peaks using the candles patters will be explained in more details in Section 5.14.

5.3 MA, SMA, EMA

In this book we use the stock indicators, RSI, MACD and SlowSTO which are explained in later sections. These indicators are calculated using MA, SMA and EMA. The purpose of this section is to explain the meaning of SMA and EMA.

MA is an abbreviation of <u>Moving Average</u>, which means an average of stock or fund prices in the past N periods. The period is a unit of time and can be different for each chart depending on the definition, but usually it is a day. N also can be different depending on the definition for a chart, but N=14 is most often used.

MA has two versions, one is SMA and another EMA. SMA means <u>Simple Moving Average</u>, which is an arithmetic average of the prices for N periods, while EMA is <u>Exponential Moving Average</u>, which is interpreted as an exponential moving average of the price in N periods, although actually it is an exponential moving average of infinite number of the past periods.

In stockcharts.com, MA and SMA are synonyms. There, MA(50) and MA(200) are overlaid in all price charts, in blue and red, respectively. They are named 50-day moving average and 200-day moving average, respectively. However, they can be changed to EMA if desired.

SMA and EMA are both used as foundation of other stock price indicators. EMA is used when MACD is computed. SMA and EMA are also used by themselves as stock price indicators. When EMS ascends, the stock price is in the trend of ascending even though the stock price fluctuates. In the same token, if EMA descends, the stock price is in the trend of descending.

The equation to compute SMA is given by

$$SMA = (\text{sum of closing prices during N periods})/N \quad (1)$$

EMA is calculated as follows. Assuming that N=10,

$$\text{EMA(today)} = [\text{Price(today)} - \text{EMA (yesterday)}]*W$$
$$+ \text{EMA (yesterday)}$$
$$= \text{Price(today)}*W + \text{EMA(yesterday)}*(1-W) \qquad (2)$$

where "*" is a multiplication operator, same as "x", and

$$W = [2/(N+1)] = [2 \div (10+1)] = 0.1818 \text{ or } 18.18\% \qquad (3)$$

We pursue the meaning of Eq. (2) rigorously further. We first point out that the equation for W, namely $W = [2 \div (N+1)]$, is an empirical formula. It is just a matter of convenience and tradition. The users of EMA have been using $W = [2 \div (N+1)]$ for a long time. Therefore, a different choice of W will cause confusion.

Figure 5.10 Example of EMA (10) and EMA (2) (stockcharts.com)

The EMA based on the definition of W=2/(N+1) is written as EMA(N), for example, EMA with N=10 is EMA(10), and that with N=20 is EMA(20). In the Figure 5.10, the definitions of the black and red curves are given at the left upper part of the graph of the stock price. Although black and red cannot be differentiated in a book printed in black/white, the black curves are a little thicker than the red curves. Notice also, depending on the choice of the user of the graph, SMA or simply MA may be plotted in place of EMA.

Equation (2) to calculate EMA may be written as

$$\begin{aligned}\text{EMA(today)} &= \text{Price(today)}*W + \text{EMA(yesterday)}*(1-W) \\ &= \text{Price(today)}*W + \text{Price(yesterday)}*W*(1-W) \\ &\quad + \text{EMA(2days ago)} \times (1-W)^2 \\ &= \text{Price(today)}*W + \text{Price(yesterday)}*W*(1-W) \\ &\quad + \text{Price(2days ago)}*W*(1-W)^2 + \text{EMA(3days ago)}*(1-W)^3 \\ &= \text{Price(today)}*W + \text{Price(yesterday)}*W*(1-W) \\ &\quad + \text{Price(2days ago)}*W*(1-W)^2 + \ldots \\ &\quad + \text{Price(N-1 days ago)}*W*(1-W)^{N-1} \\ &\quad + \text{EMA(N days ago)}*(1-W)^N \quad\quad (4)\end{aligned}$$

In the prior equation, W, $W(1-W)$, $W(1-W)^2$, ... $W*(1-W)^{N-1}$ are the weights for the past N prices. If all the prices are 1 and EMA(N days ago) is 1, the total of the weight must become 1.

To make sure this is true, we set

$$\text{Price(today)} = \text{Price(yesterday)} = \ldots = \text{Price(N-1)}$$
$$= \text{EMA(N days ago)} = 1 \quad\quad (5)$$

and rewrite Equation (4). Then, we get

$$\begin{aligned}\text{EMA(today)} &= W + W*(1-W) + W*(1-W)^2 + \\ &\quad + W*(1-W)^{N-1} + (1-W)^N \\ &= W[\,1 + (1-W) + (1-W)^2 + \ldots + (1-W)^{N-1}\,] \\ &\quad + (1-W)^N \quad\quad (6)\end{aligned}$$

Now, using a standard formula to calculate the sum of a power series,

$$1 + r + r^2 + r^3 + \ldots r^N = (1 - r^{(N+1)})/(1 - r) \quad (7)$$

and rewriting Eq.(6) yields

$$\begin{aligned} \text{EMA(today)} &= W[\,1 + (1\text{-}W) + (1\text{-}W)^2 + \ldots + (1 - W)^{N\text{-}1}\,] + (1\text{-}W)^N \\ &= W[\,1 - (1\text{-}W)^N\,]/[\,1 - (1\text{-}W)\,] + (1\text{-}W)^N \\ &= [\,1 - (1\text{-}W)^N\,] + (1\text{-}W)^N \\ &= 1 \quad (8) \end{aligned}$$

We confirmed that the total of the weights becomes 1.

Figure 5.11 is a plot of the weights for N=10.

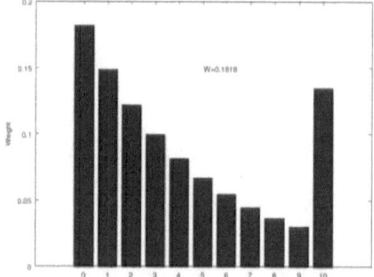

Figure 5.11 Distribution of weights (N=10)

It is seen that the weight for the last term is unexpectedly high. The weights of the first 10 are certainly the weights for the prices of the 10 days, but the last one is for the weight beyond the 10 days.

We now artificially double the value of W and plot in Figure 5.10.

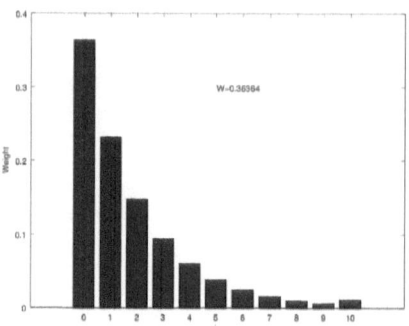

Figure 5.12 Distribution of weights (N=10) where W of Figure 5.9 is artificially doubled

In Figure 5.12, the weight for the first place, namely the weight for the latest closing price is doubled, but the last one is drastically decreased.

Let us investigate more in depth the meaning of the term $(1-W)^N$EMA(N days ago), so we replace "today" in Equation (4) by "N days ago" and get:

EMA(N days ago) =

$= $ Price(N days ago)$*W + $ EMA(N+1 days ago)$*(1-W)$

$= $ Price(N days ago)$*W + $ Price(N+1 days ago)$*W*(1-W)$

$+ $ Price(N+2 days ago)$*W*(1-W)^2 + $

$+ $ Price(2N-1 days ago)$*W*(1-W)^{N-1}$

$+ $ EMA(2N days ago)$*(1-W)^N$ (9)

If we substitute this in Eq.(4), we get

EMA(today) =
Price(today)$*W + $ Price(yesterday)$*W*(1-W)$

$+ $ Price(2days ago)$*W*(1-W)^2 + ...$

$+ $ Price(N-1 days ago)$*W*(1-W)^{N-1}$

$+ $ EMA(N days ago)$*(1-W)^N$

$= $ Price(today)$*W + $ Price(yesterday)$*W*(1-W)$

$+ $ Price(2days ago)$*W*(1-W)^2 + ...$

$+ $ Price(N-1 days ago)$*W*(1-W)^{N-1}$

$+ $ Price(N days ago)$*W*(1-W)^N$

$+ $ Price(N+1 days ago)$*W*(1-W)^{N+1} + ...$

$+ $ EMA(2N days ago)$*(1-W)^{2N}$ (10)

By repeating this, the equation for EMA becomes the summation of an infinite series, regardless of N. That is, EMA is a weighted sum of an infinite series of prices regardless of N.

In Eq. (10), the only influence of N is through the equation $W=2/(N+1)$. EMA is not a weighted sum of the prices in N periods. This explanation does not agree with many other literatures: we can say, they do not understand the foregoing mathematical analysis, and they are wrong.

The only way that N influences EMA is by W=2/(N+1). We are interested in how the distribution of weights changes by N. The weight distributions are plotted for three different values of N, namely N=5, 10, and 20, in Figures 5.13, 5.14, and 5.15, respectively.

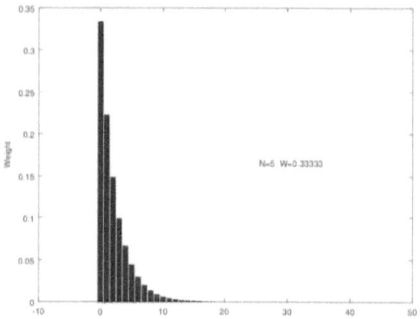

Figure 5.13   Weight distribution for N=5

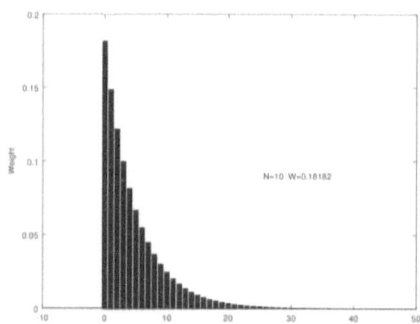

Figure 5.14   Weight distributions for N=10

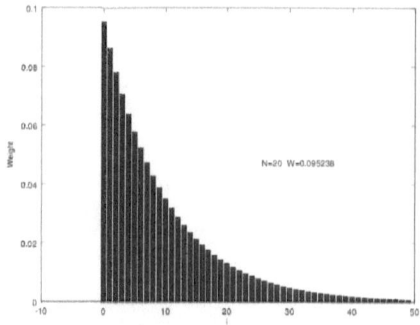

Figure 5.15   Weight distributions for N=20

EMA is used in many other applications. In order to signify that an EMA is a weighted average of N data, W is determined in some applications so that EMA(N days ago)*(1–W)^N in Eq.(4) becomes negligibly small. For example, in order that its weight, $(1 - W)^N$, becomes less than 0.1%, W can be determined by solving the equation, $(1-W)^N = 0.001$. If N=10, then $1 - W = (0.001)^{1/10} = 0.5011$. Solving this equation yields W=0.4988. By revising Fig. 5.9, we get Fig. 5.14.

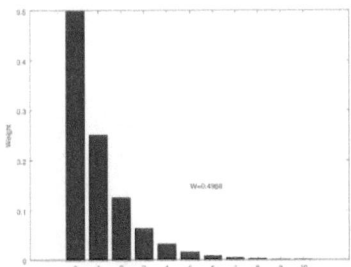

Figure 5.14   Fig.5.9 is revised with W=0.4988

In Fig. 5.14, the last weight is 0.1% and negligibly small, but earlier weights became much higher than in Fig. 5.8, and comparable to Fig. 5.9 in which N=5 and W=2/(N+1) are used.

The weighted average obtained in this way is nearly equal to the weighted average of exactly 10 days. But when applied to the analysis of stock prices, it yields different results than the traditional way.

In conclusion, the explanation that "EMA with N=14, for example, is a exponential average of the prices in 14 periods" is wrong. The truth is that EMA using N=14 is an exponential average of the past infinite number of prices using W=2/(N+1). However, there is nothing wrong in using EMA(N) as a stock price indicator, so there is no need to change the way to used EMA(N).

Wise men go along with the majority after understanding everything.

5.4 RSI

RSI is an abbreviation of <u>Relative Strength Index</u> which is an oscillator that moves like a momentum oscillator. Moving between 0 and 100, RSI indicates the velocity and magnitude of the price movements. When RSI exceeds 70, the stock is considered <u>overbought</u> (by the investors), and when it is less than 30, the stock is considered <u>oversold</u>. Therefore, when RSI is greater than 70 and makes a peak, it is the time to sell, and when RSI is less than 30 and makes a bottom, it is the time to buy.

Figure 5.15 is a price chart of DOWJ from November 2016 to February of 2019. RSI is plotted above the price chart. Stock market in 2918 had two major corrections, one starting in February and another starting in October. Look at RSI during October 2018 to February 2018. RSI started rising in October 2017 and peaked in February 2018. The RSI value at the peak of February 2018 was extremely high. At the second correction in 2018 starting in October 2018, RSI was not as high as in February but the DOWJ index was nearly the same. At this time of writing this paragraph on 3 March 2019, RSI is rising again but the DOWJ index is again approaching the peaks in February 2018 and October 2018.

Figure 5.17   Chart of DOWJ with a plot of RSI

22

Figures 5.18 and 5.19 show price charts of JNUG on 20 July 2018 and 24 August 2018, respectively, using stockcharts.com. RSI is plotted at the top of the chart. See on Fig. 5.18 that RSI exceeds 70 two times, but soon after those peaks, the price started descending. These are examples of that, if RSI exceeds 70, it is time to sell the stock or fund. In Fig.5.16, RSI became less than 30, which indicates the price became close to a bottom, and the time to buy at the bottom is near.

Figure 5.18   Price chart of JNUG on 20 July 2018

Figure 5.19   Price chart of JNUG on 24 Aug 2018

With RSI alone, however, we may miss opportunities to buy and sell because RSI is not perfect to catch the timings of buy and sell. In other words, RSI may not become below 30 when the time is the real buying opportunity, or RSI may not exceed 70 when the time is a real selling opportunity. Another possible problem with RSI is that, even when RSI is below 30, it may continue to stay under 30 and does not form a clear bottom. An opposite can happen such that RSI exceeds 70 but stays there for a long time and a clear top is not formed. This is the reason why we need other indicators such as MACDS and SlowSTO, which are explained later.

One important role of RSI, however, is that it may show divergence. The word "divergence" refers to certain slopes of the price movements. If the slope of RSI is ascending but the slope of the stock price is descending, it is divergence. An opposite type of divergence can happen such that the slope of RSI is descending but the slope of prices is ascending. Either way, if a divergence is observed, it is the time exercise caution, because the direction of the stock price movement may change suddenly to the direction of the slope of RSI.

Figure 5.20 Example of divergence between price and RSI

5.5 Method of Computing RSI

Calculation of RSI needs past data of closing prices, and to specify how many periods of the past, N, is to be used. The default value of N is 14 when no particular value is given. The period definition is normally a day, but can be 1 hour or week, or any other length of time. We assume here that the period is a day. We define a gain as the increase of price if the price goes up from the last period to the present period. Likewise a loss is the decrease of price if the price goes down. The gain for the period is set to 0 if the price change is negative. Also, the loss is set to zero if the change is positive. The average gain in N periods is the total of the gains during N periods divided by N. Likewise the average loss is the total of losses in N period divided by N.

In Table 5.1, the 2nd column is the stock price of 20 periods. Column 3 is the gains with plus sign and losses with minus sign. Columns 4 and 5 are copies of the gains and losses, respectively.

Starting at the 15th row, column 6 is the average gains in N periods, column 7 is the average losses. Column 8 and 9 are exponential averages (explained in the next paragraph) of gain and losses. In row 15, exponential average cannot be calculated, so the same values of column 6 and 7, respectively, are written.

Table 5.1   Example of calculations of RS and RSI

Period	Closing	Change	Gain	Loss	Simple avgain	Simple avloss	Smooth avgain	Smooth avloss	RS	RSI
1	46.125	N/A								
2	47.125	1.000	1.000							
3	46.438	-0.688		0.688						
4	46.938	0.500	0.500							
5	44.938	-2.000		2.000						
6	44.250	-0.688		0.688						
7	44.626	0.376	0.376							
8	45.750	1.124	1.124							
9	47.812	2.062	2.062							
10	47.562	-0.249		0.249						
11	47.000	-0.562		0.562						
12	44.562	-2.438		2.438						
13	46.312	1.750	1.750							
14	47.688	1.375	1.375							
15	46.688	-1.000	0.000	1.000	0.585	0.545	0.585	0.545	1.074	51.78
16	45.688	-1.000	0.000	1.000	0.513	0.616	0.543	0.577	0.941	48.48
17	43.062	-2.625	0.000	2.625	0.513	0.754	0.504	0.723	0.697	41.07
18	43.563	0.500	0.500	0.000	0.513	0.754	0.504	0.672	0.750	42.86
19	44.876	1.313	1.313	0.000	0.607	0.612	0.562	0.624	0.901	47.38
20	43.688	-1.188	0.000	1.188	0.607	0.647	0.522	0.664	0.785	43.99

The smoothed average gain, abbreviated as "smooth avgain" in the foregoing table is calculated as

Smoothed average gain =(smoothed averaged gain of the previous period (N-1) + gain of the current period)/N

For N=14,

Smoothed average gain = (0.585 x (13) + 0.0)/14 = 0.543

Similarly,

Smoothed average loss = (smoothed average loss of the previous period*(N-1) + loss of the current period)/N

For the period 16,

Smoothed average loss = (0.545 x (13) + 1.0)/14 = 0.577

Next, RS (relative strength) is calculated by

RS = (smoothed average gain)/(smoothed average loss)

For the period 16,

RS = 0.543/0.577 = 0.941

Finally, RSI is

RSI = 100 x RS/(1+RS)

This equation may be equivalently written as

RSI = 100 x [smoothed average gain]/[smoothed average gain + smoothed average loss]

For the 16th period,

RSI = 100x0.941/(1+0.941) = 48.48

Figure 5.18 is a price chart of JNUG on 17 July 2018 by stockcharts.com. A graph of RSI with N=14 is plotted above the price chart.

Figure 5.21 Chart of JNUG on 21 Dec 2018 (stockcharts.com)
RSI is plotted above the price chart

If RSI<30, the stock is considered to be oversold, while if RSI>70 it is considered to be overbought. The RSI graph in Figure 5.21 indicates that RSI became under 30 on 10 August 2018, that is JNUG is oversold, and a bottom was reached around 15 August 2018. Another bottom is reached on 11 September 2018 when RSI made a dip below 30. If bought while RSI is above 30, there were some chances that the price further goes down. Likewise, if sold while RSI is below 70, there were some chances that the price goes up, respectively

RSI is not a perfect indicator. Indeed, it often misses good timing of both buy and sell. Nevertheless it is a good indicator when combined with other indicators.

5.6 MACD

MACD (pronounced like "mak" or "mak dee") is an abbreviation of Moving Average Convergence Divergence indicator, which is a trend-following momentum indicator. MACD is based on two moving averages of stock/fund prices.

A MACD graph has two curves (black and red)[3] plus one histogram (blue) as illustrated in the bottom of Figure 5.22. The black curve is MACD itself (thick curve in black/white print), red is the signal line (thin in black/white print), the histogram (blue bars) is the difference between MACD and signal line.

Figure 5.22 Price chart of SOXL with RSI and MACD

Notice that there is a print, "MACD (12, 26, 9)", on the left side of the MACD graph. The three numbers, 12, 26, 9, are parameters used in computing the MACD, which can be changed by the user. The numbers 12, 26 and 9 are default.

MACD (thick curve) has the following features. The curve of MACD is similar to the price movement but is smoother than the price movement. When the trend of price movement is upward, MACD (black curve) moves upward above the thin line, named Signal Line. On the other hand, in a bear (downward) trend of the price, MACD (thick curve) moves downward under the thin line.

The point of time when the black curve crosses the red line is <u>an important time</u>. The black curve crosses from under the red line upward, when the stock price has passed a bottom. Similarly, the black line crosses from above the red line downward, when the stock price has passed a peak.

---

[3] In a book printed in black ink only, the colors of the curves cannot be identified except by thickness. The reader are suggested to open stckcharts.com and plot price charts by themselves and have a close loot at.

Some investors buy the stock when the former occurs, or sell when the latter occurs. However, those crosses often delay a few days compared to the optimum timing of selling or buying.

Sometimes, this delay not only diminishes the potential of profit, but can cause a loss if the stock price moves fast. This delay can be decreased by changing the parameters (12, 26, 9) to (6, 13, 5), for example.

Another way to decrease the effect of delayed timing is as follows. Notice that the timing of a price bottom or peak agree with the bottom or peak of the histogram in blue. Therefore, after confirming the formation of bottom or peak of the blue histogram, buying or selling can be executed without waiting for the time of crossing.

However, a delay of buy or selling is not always bad, because by confirming the formation of bottom or peak with a delay, the risk of making a mistake may well be reduced.

Another advantage of MACD may occur when holding a stock. The price movements can be sluggish with up and down. When the stock price goes down, the investor's confidence for holding the stock is often shaken. In such a case, look at the MACD movement. If the black line is ascending upward above the red curve, the stock is in bull trend despite a temporary bear day.

Sometimes the trend of price and that of MACD diverge, which often indicate that the trend of price movement will change in a near future.

5.7 Calculation of MACD

MACD (black curve) and Signal line (red curve) are calculated by the following equations, assuming the parameters are 12, 26, and 9:

$$\text{MACD (black)} = \text{EMA}(12) - \text{EMA}(26)$$

$$\text{Signal line (red)} = \text{EMA}(9)$$

Histogram is calculated by subtracting Signal line from MACD:

$$\text{Histogram} = \text{MACD (black curve)} - \text{Signal line (red curve)}$$

Here, EMA(26), EMA(26) and EMA(9) are exponential moving average using N=12, 26, and 9, respectively. The meaning of N was explained in Section 5.3. These numbers are combined in the argument of MACD, for example MACD(12, 26, 9), as use in Figure 5.20.

The combination of the three parameters, (12, 26, 9), is most widely used but not necessarily the best combination. In case the stock price moves fast, a combination of smaller numbers, for example (6, 13, 5), may work better. If stockcharts.com is used to plot a stock chart, the parameters can be changed as the user wishes. However, changing the parameter for different times or different fund/stock require cumbersome operations. We rather would use a fixed set of parameters, and try to understand when MACD works or not.

When to look at a MACD graph, we need to examine at the right end of the graph to find out:
(1) if the black and red curves are both ascending, or descending,
(2) if the black and read curves are crossing,
(3) if the histogram just passed a peak on the positive side,
(4) if the histogram just passed a bottom on the negative side
(5) if the histogram is very close to zero.
(6) if the black line is running above the red curve when the black curve is ascending,
(7) if the black curve is running below the red curve when the black curve is descending.

An examination of Figure 5.23 to answer the foregoing questions is left for the reader's exercise.

Figure 5.23 The stock chart for SOXL with MACD(12, 26, 9)

MACD is a useful and powerful tool, but by no means a perfect tool. It has no power to predict unexpected price movements. Also, it looses the power after sudden price movements.

MACD is most useful in determining of buy/sell timings when combined with the information from RSI and SlowSTO indicators.

If the investor judges the timings of buy/sell primarily by the shapes and combinations of candles as explained in 5.13, MACD should help identifying the time approaching a peak or a bottom.

5.8 Divergence of MACD

The divergence of MACD is that the slope of MACD movement and that of the stock/fund price are opposite to each other. If a divergence occurs, the slope of the stock/fund price tend to change to the direction of MACD in the near future.

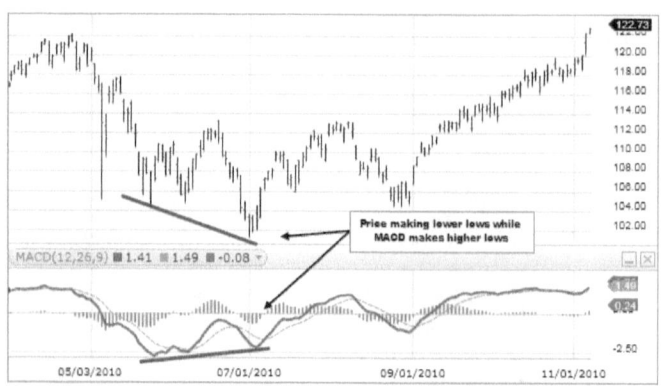
Figure 5.24 Example of divergence between the price movement of MACD

We now investigate how the parameters, for example (12, 26, 9) in MACD(12, 26, 9), affect the graph of MACD. Figure 5.25 and 5.26 show the MACD plots of (12, 26, 9) and (6, 13, 5), respectively.

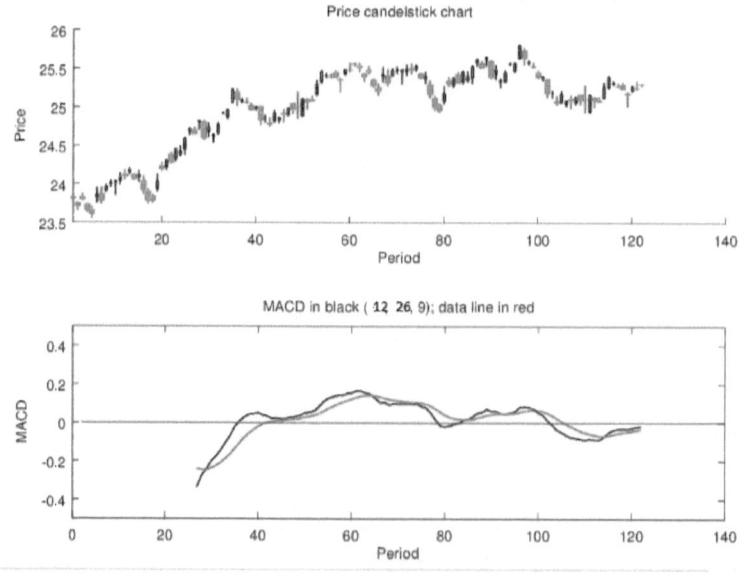

Figure 5.25 Price movement (the upper graph) and MACD(12, 26, 9) (the lower graph)

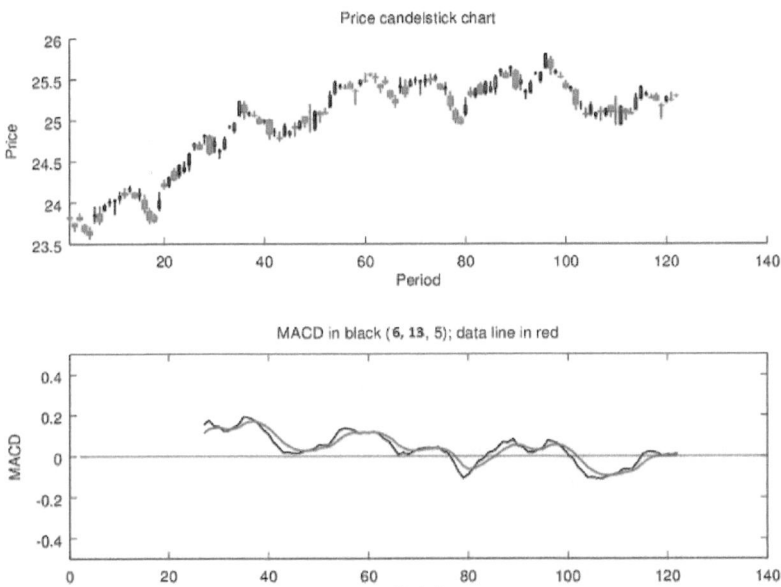

Figure 5.26 Price movement (the upper graph) and MACD(6, 13, 5) (the lower graph)

Comparing Figures 5.25 and 5.26, the latter has many more intersections between the black and red curves. In the left end of the chart, MACD in Figure 5.25 is rising, but in Figure 5.26, MACD is descending with divergence from the stock price. This means that for short trading, MACD (6, 13, 5) is more suitable than MACD(12, 26, 9) because it predicts the change in the direction of price movement.

Figure 5.27 is a price chart of UWT. In this example, price peaks and bottoms are well rendered by the histogram. The crosses of black and red are too much delayed except once.

Figure 5.27 Price chart of UWT

As another example, Figure 5.28 is a chart of JNUG, in which the bottoms and peaks are well captured by the histogram.

Figure 5.28 Price chart of JNUG

5.9 FastSTO Indicator

FastSTO is an abbreviation of Fast Stochastic Oscilator, which was developed in 1950's by George Lane. It is used as a stock price indicator along with RSI and MACD.

FastSTO is calculated by

$$\%K = 100*(C-L_N)/(H_N-L_N)$$

where

%K is the FastSTO indicator
N is set to 14 usually, but 9 or 5 are often used
C = the latest stock price
L_N = the lowest price during the N periods
H_N = the highest price during the N periods

An associated indictor %D is defined by

$$\%D = 3\text{-day SMA of }\%K$$

Here SMA means the simple arithmetic average. Both %K and %D oscillate between 0 and 100 and plotted together.

Table 5.2 illustrates calculations of %K and %D. %K has the following meaning. In a bull market, the closing price is close to the highest price in the period, and on the other hand in a bear market, the closing price is close to the lowest in the period. The buy timing is indicated when %K crosses %D from below. On the other hand, the timing of sell is when %K crosses %D from above.

Table 5.2 Illustration for calculations of FastSTO

	Date	High	Low	Highest High (14)	Lowest Low (14)	Current Close	14-day Stochastic Oscillator
1	23-Feb-10	127.01	125.36				
2	24-Feb-10	127.62	126.16				
3	25-Feb-10	126.59	124.93				
4	26-Feb-10	127.35	126.09				
5	1-Mar-10	128.17	126.82				
6	2-Mar-10	128.43	126.48				
7	3-Mar-10	127.37	126.03				
8	4-Mar-10	126.42	124.83				
9	5-Mar-10	126.90	126.39				
10	8-Mar-10	126.85	125.72				
11	9-Mar-10	125.65	124.56				
12	10-Mar-10	125.72	124.57				
13	11-Mar-10	127.16	125.07				
14	12-Mar-10	127.72	126.86	128.43	124.56	127.29	70.44
15	15-Mar-10	127.69	126.63	128.43	124.56	127.18	67.61
16	16-Mar-10	128.22	126.80	128.43	124.56	128.01	89.20
17	17-Mar-10	128.27	126.71	128.43	124.56	127.11	65.81
18	18-Mar-10	128.09	126.80	128.43	124.56	127.73	81.75
19	19-Mar-10	128.27	126.13	128.43	124.56	127.06	64.52
20	22-Mar-10	127.74	125.92	128.27	124.56	127.33	74.53
21	23-Mar-10	128.77	126.99	128.77	124.56	128.71	98.58
22	24-Mar-10	129.29	127.81	129.29	124.56	127.87	70.10
23	25-Mar-10	130.06	128.47	130.06	124.56	128.58	73.06
24	26-Mar-10	129.12	128.06	130.06	124.56	128.60	73.42
25	29-Mar-10	129.29	127.61	130.06	124.57	127.93	61.23
26	30-Mar-10	128.47	127.60	130.06	125.07	128.11	60.96
27	31-Mar-10	128.09	127.00	130.06	125.92	127.60	40.39
28	1-Apr-10	128.65	126.90	130.06	125.92	127.60	40.39

Because of its too fast oscillation of FastSTO hinders its usefulness, an improved version named SlowSTO is far more useful than FastSTO.

5.10 SlowSTO Indicator

SlowSTO is an abbreviation of Slow Stochastic Oscilator, and more powerful than RSI and MACD in many ways, although it is not a perfect indicator. In fact, some times it fails while RSI or MACD works better, The best way is to make judgment using all three of RSI, MACD and SlowSTO.

SlowSTO is denoted by two quantities, one is %K or %K(N) in black color and another is an associated quantity %D in red color, where N is the number of periods on which the calculation is based. The colors of %K and %D cannot be identified in black/white print, but %K is thicker than %D.

Their mathematical formula are written as

%K= 100x[Average of (C-L_N) in M periods / average of

(H_N–L_N) in M periods]

%D = SMA of Slow %K

where,

C = Last closing price
L_N = Lowest price during the N period
H_N = Maximum price during the N period
M = Number of periods in which %K is averaged to calculate %D

Normally N=14 and M=3 are used, but other values may be used as well.

Figure 5.26 is a price chart of UWT including MACD, SlowSTO, and FastSTO. In Figure 5.26, it is seen that SlowSTO is similar to FastSTO, but smoother and has less fluctuations when the indicators are above 80 or below 20. The time to sell is near when the indicators pass the line of 80 from below, and the time to buy is near when the indicators pass the line of 20 from above. The optimum time to sell is when both black(thick) and red(thin) curves are above 80, and the black curve is crossing the red curve from above. This occurs after both curves cross the line of 80 upward but before they pass the line of 80 downward. Conversely, the optimum time to buy is when both black and red curves are below 20, and the black (thick) curve passes the red (thin) curve from below. SlowSTO renders the buy/sell timings more frequently than MACD when the price oscillations are relatively fast.

However, the rules in the prior paragraph are not applicable if the red curve and black curve cross each other multiple times, which occur often the interval that SlowSTO stays above 80 for a long period, or SlowSTO stays below 20 for a long period. In such a case, look at the histogram of MACD. The time the histogram on the negative side becomes the maximum in length is the optimum time to buy. Also, the time the histogram on the positive side becomes the maximum in length is the optimum time to sell.

In any case try to sell or buy with a best effort to wait for a peak or bottom to form, because timing the truly optimum moment to buy or sell is impossible. Therefore, a small loss may occur right after you buy or sell. That is the nature of trading in stock market.

The investor is suggested to examine in the stock chart on how SlowSTO depicts the timing of buy and sell for the fund or stock in which the investor is interested.

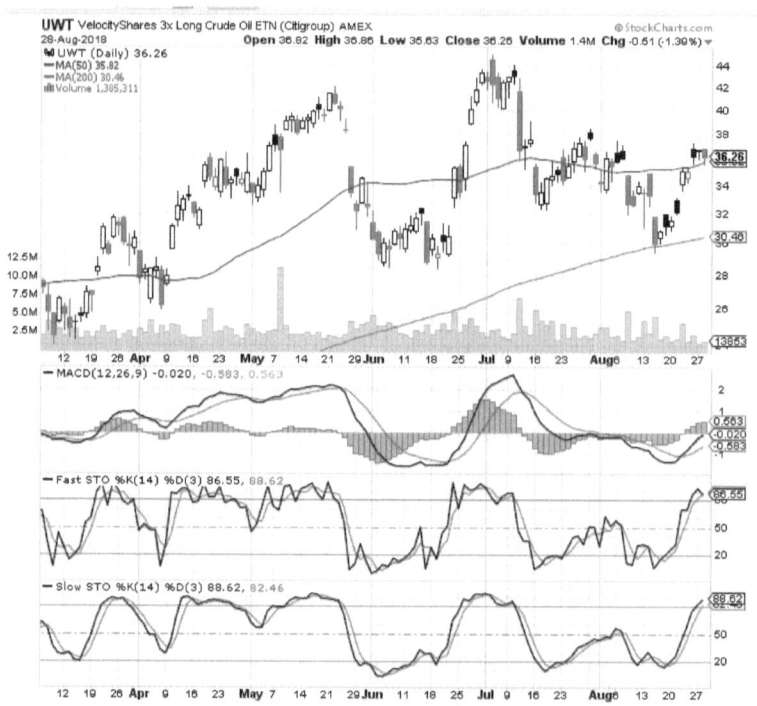

Figure 5.29 Price chart of UWT including MACD, SlowSTO, FastSTO

One example of good prediction of selling time by SlowSTO is Illustrated in Figure 5.30.

Figure 5.30 Price chart of JNUG with SlowSTO

In Figure 5.30, the peaks are mostly clearly depicted by SlowSTO. Some bottoms are also clearly shown. However, during the period of 9 July 2018 to 9 September, the values of SlowSTO was continuously under 30, and did not tell any good timing to buy or sell. The descending movement of JNUG was far better rendered by MACD's histogram and RSI. The bottom on 15 August 2018 was clearly depicted by RSI. This chart indicates that looking at the price chart is the most important in making decisions of buy/sell with the aids of the three price indicators.

On the other hand, if JDST (bear counter part of JNUG) was bought on 9 July 2018, then MACD showed good selling timing of 15 August 2018. During this period MACD descended showing that JNUG was continuously descending, or equivalently JDST was continuously ascending. See also, during this continuously descending period of JNUG, SlowSTO was almost continuously under 20. This is an example of the time that SlowSTO for JDST continuously exceeded 80 but did not indicate a good timing of selling on 15 August 2018.

If the behavior of MACD and that of SlowSTO are compared, MACD tends to smooth out small peaks and bottoms, but renders long term trend of the price movements better than SlowSTO. This helps trading during a continuously ascending market or continuously descending market. On the other hand, SlowSTO renders short term peaks and bottoms more clearly than MACD. Therefore, for trading at each peak and bottom by ignoring long term trend, SlowSTO may be more useful.

5.11 What the Indicators Do Not Do Well

In Figure 5.31, the price peaks that are circled by hand writing are not well depicted by any of the indicators so the investors may have missed to take appropriate actions if the indictors are strictly relied on.

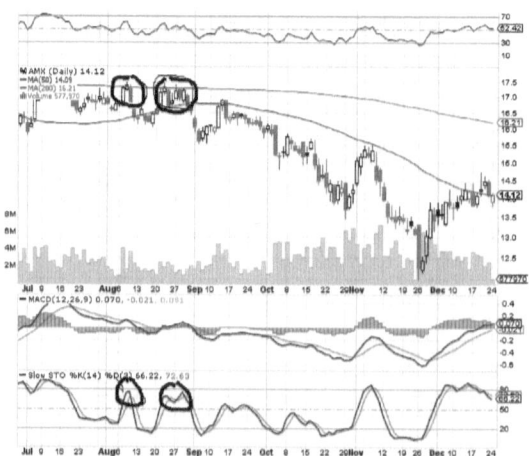

Figure 5.31 Chart of AMX

Figure 5.32 Chat of SPX

In Figure 5.32, the peak, which was important to the investors, marked by hand written circles, was poorly depicted by SlowSTO, nor RSI and MACD.

Figure 5.33 Chart of TNA

In Figure 5.33, the last peak (1 December 2018) before the big descend in December, marked by handwritten circles, was poorly depicted by SlowSTO. Selling at that point was important if TNA was bought on 19 November 2018. Also it was an extremely important time if TNZ, the bear counterpart of TNA, was to be bought.

This example tells us that the peaks of SlowSTO need to re observed even when it is below the line of 80. The peak on 1 December 2018 was clearly indicated in the histogram of MACD. However, if the investor was well aware that the market was in a severe down trend judging from the decending trend that started in September 2018, the importance of paying attention to the peak on 1 December 2018 could have been realized by watching the slope of MA(50) overlaid on the price chart.

A low peak like the once circled in Figure 5.33 tends to occur when the market is in down trend. The investor should check if the market is up-trend or down-trend from the price chart and the slope of MA curve overlaid in the price chart.

Figure 5.34 Chart of DGX

In Figure 5.34, two small bottoms in October were overemphasized by RSI. Also the peak circled by hand writing before a large slide toward the year end was poorly depicted by SlowSTO. Like the case of Figure 5.30, the investor should have been aware that this peak occurred during the continuously descending period. Any peak that appears in a descending market may be a good time to buy more bear funds.

Figure 5.35 Price chart of SOXL

As seen in Figured 5.35, a serious decline of SOXL started around 1 October 2018. But none of RSI, MACD and SlowSTO indicated seriousness of the decline that lasted until the end of 2018. Investors would wish to be notified about the start of rapid decline on 1 October 2018.

If the investor bought SOXL about 10 October 2018 at the signal of SlowSTO that went below 20, then SlowSTO did not generate any good signal for selling. After ascending for a few days, SOXL started going down severely. The investor must have checked the market condition by looking at the price movement in the recent past.

If the market is in a strongly descending trend, the condition will generally last for some long time to come. Therefore, frequent buy/sell in accordance to the peaks and bottoms of SlowSTO is harmful. The down trend of the market could have been seen in the slope of MA(50) overlaid in the price chart.

The most profitable action during the strong downturn like this was to buy SOXS, the bear counterpart of SOXL, and hold until the very bottom was reached, like 24 December 2018.

Figure 5.36 Price chart of DOWJ

In Figure 5.36, the peak on 1 October is poorly rendered by RSI. Also the peak in early December, which was the last peak before the severe decline in December, was not depicted well by SlowSTO.

As shown in the foregoing examples, the indicators are not perfect. That means, if we strictly depend on the indicators, we miss some important timings. Of course, we cannot blame the indicators, because predicting the future by the indicators are all based on mathematical process of the past data. We thank the indicators for good performance in most of times, but it is important to use our own judgment when the indicators do not work well.

Another pattern of the price movements where SlowSTO fails is when the price ascends for an extended period, or when the price descends for an extended period. In the former case, SlowSTO exceeds 80 but stay there for a long period. There are many examples in the SlowSTO charts in this book The first examples are in Figure 5.33. Look at the period in July to September. Three major time intervals where SlowSTO mostly stayed above 80 are seen. None of these intervals included a good time to sell except the end of the three.

An example of SlowSTo staying below 20 is seen in Figure 5.27. The period under 20 lasted almost a month starting on 16 July 2018. This example indicates that the time that SlowSTO entering the region user 20 cannot be interpreted as a buying opportunity particularly if the market is in a descending trend. Many more similar examples can found in this book.

Repeating for summary, don't jump into buying or selling by only SlowSTO's coming down to 20 or below, or into selling by only SlowSTO's going up to 80 or above.

5.12 Is the Market in Up Trend or Down Trend?

This question can be answered easily by looking at the price chart and see if the price is downward or upward. If the market is downward, MACD is moving downward. If the market is upward, just the opposite can be observed. MA(50), which is overlaid in the price chart, moves upward in an ascending market, or downward in an descending market. When the market moves upward for an extended period, SlowSTO tends to stay above 80 continuously, and likewise, when the market moves downward for an extended period, SlowSTO tends to stay below 20 continuously.

If the market is moving upward strongly, the investor does not need to look at SlowSTO or MACD, but just buy bull fund. Likewise, If the market is downward strongly, the investor does not need to look at SlowSTO or MACD, but just buy bear fund.

5.13 Advanced/Decline Line Indicator

Advance/decline line indicator, abbreviated by AD line, is an early warning indicator. The AD Line indicator tells whether a great bull market is still full of energy, or when the market starts to wear out. Conversely it tells whether a bear market is still losing energy further, or when the market to restart ascending. An AD line plot can be created with stockcharts.com as illustrated later in this section.

When the bull market is going strong, the number of stocks gaining a higher price becomes larger than the number of stocks losing price. But as prices nears the peak, fewer stocks gains.

The advance/decline line looks at how many stocks in a specified stock market (such as NY stock exchange) went up in a day versus how many went down. If more stocks rise than fall in a day, then the advance/decline line will rise by the difference. Conversely if more stocks fall than rise in a day, the AD line will fall by the difference.

It's a great way to see how strong the stock market really is. If more stocks are rising than falling, then it tells us the current bull market is broad-based.

In the middle of February 2019, the advance/decline line broke out to new all-time highs.

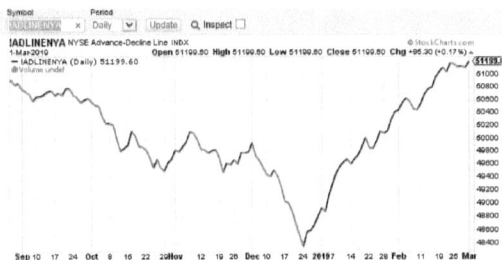

Figure 5.37 A sample of AD line chart for NY Stock Exchange

Figure 5.38 Parameters used in creating Figure 5.37

The AD Line indicator in Figure 5.37 hit new highs toward the end of February 2019. We saw major rallies in stocks across the board again and it seemed that the bull market wasn't over yet.

However, since the beginning of March 2019, the AD Line has not hit new highs, but rather it is declining indicating that the market got into a bear trend. On March 8, not only prices of many bull ETF declined but also TVIX ascended significantly and prices of bear ETFs went up.

To get an AD line indicator plotted, open stockcharts.com first. Type in a box for symbol (at the top left corner of the site), "advance decline line" without quote signs and click on an update button. Then, a table that looks like below opens:

Table 5.3 Options in choosing a different AD Line
(only a part of the table is shown)

Symbol		Name	Exch	Sector	Industry	First Data Point	Mention
⌇ ▦ ₀⅗ ✳ ❶	!ADLINEDOW	DOW Advance-Decline Line	INDX			1998-06-15	💬
⌇ ▦ ₀⅗ ✳ ❶	!ADLINESPX	SPX Advance-Decline Line	INDX			1998-10-07	💬
⌇ ▦ ₀⅗ ✳ ❶	!ADLINENDX	NDX Advance-Decline Line	INDX			1998-10-07	💬
⌇ ▦ ₀⅗ ✳ ❶	!ADLINENYA	NYSE Advance-Decline Line	INDX			1926-01-02	💬
⌇ ▦ ₀⅗ ✳ ❶	!ADLINENAS	NASDAQ Advance-Decline Line	INDX			1978-01-03	💬

Click on the leftmost icon on the line of NYSE Advance-Decline Line. Then, a chart similar to Figure 5.37 opens. To finalize the figure, some parameters must be adjusted as illustrated in Figure 5.38.

The AD line can be plotted for other stock market indices such as DOWJ, SPX, NASDAQ, depending on which line in the table illustrated in Table 5 is selected. It is also possible to plot of AD Lines based on the volume of stocks rather than the numbers of advance and decline.

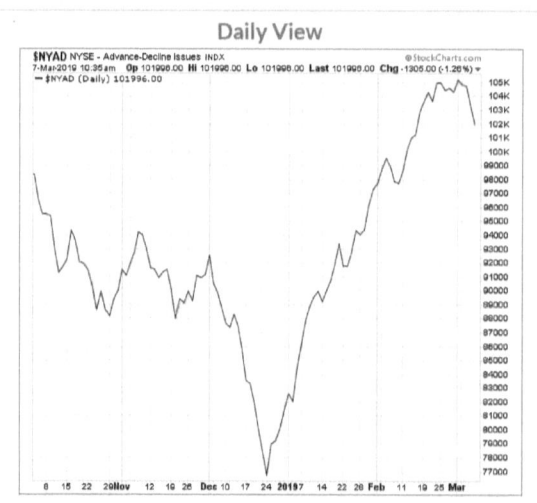

Figure 5.39 AD Line plot of NYEX on 7 March 2019

A shortcut in plotting an AD Line is to type in a symbol such as !ADLINENYA in the small window for a symbol on the price chart page of stockcharts.com.[4]

5.14 How to identify the Day of Peak and Day of Bottom

It is imperative to identify the day of peak and bottom on the day it happens. In fact, in buying a bull ETF, the best time is during the day that the price reaches the bottom and the price movement reversal occurs. Likewise, the best time to sell is during the day that the price reaches the top and the price movement reversal occurs.

The principle is essentially the same in trading a bear ETF. The best time to buy a bear ETF id when the ETF price is at the peak, and the best time to sell is when the ETF price comes to the bottom

Methods of identifying peaks and bottoms using the stock price indicators, RSI, MACD and SlowSTO cannot pin point the peaks and bottom precisely always.

This section describes how to find more precise timing of peaks and bottom using the shapes of candles in coordination with price indicators.

In this approach, we need to look at the shape of the candle of the fund you are planning to trade after the market opens in the morning and one more time before the market closes. We look at the shape of the candles every day and the candles in the past several day to find if the peak or bottom is today.

In order to explain the approach, we next observe candles shapes at peaks and bottoms of a few funds.

---

[4] The readers of this book should welcome and love declining stock market. It is a great opportunity to make money by buying TVIX and bear ETFs. On March 2019, DOWJ lost 0.45%, while TVIX gained 4.05%, JDST gained 13.13%, short selling of CHAU gained 8.1%.

Observations of the candles at peaks and bottoms

Observation of WTI price chart in Figure 5.40

a: Look at the bull candle denoted by *a* in Figure 5.40. From SlowSTO, the point *a* can be identified to be in the range of a bottom because it is below 20. The day of *a* is after a series of descending candles. It is a large bull candle following a large bear candle. This bull candle is a pivotal point. If a bear fund is to be sold, or a bull fund is to be purchased, such transactions are best to be done as soon as after the opening of the day *a*.

b: The bear candle on the day *b* is after a series of ascending candles, and has a long upper wick. On this day, the price went up to the top and descends back to the opening price, during which the candle should have been plotted as a bull candle. As it went down further, it is plotted as a bear candle. The price went down to the bottom of the lower wick and then went up to the closing price. The selling of bull fund and buying bear funds are best to be done as soon as after the price became lower than the opening price or at latest before closing of the day.

c: The day of *c* is at the bottom or close to it judging from SlowSTO. Before the day c were two descending candles. The candle at *c* became a bull candle with a long lower wick. It means that the opening price was slightly higher than the previous closing price, but the price descended during the day to the lowest of the day, and then ascended to the highest of the day before coming back to the closing price. If selling a bear fund or buying a bull fund was to be done, the best time was before closing of the day.

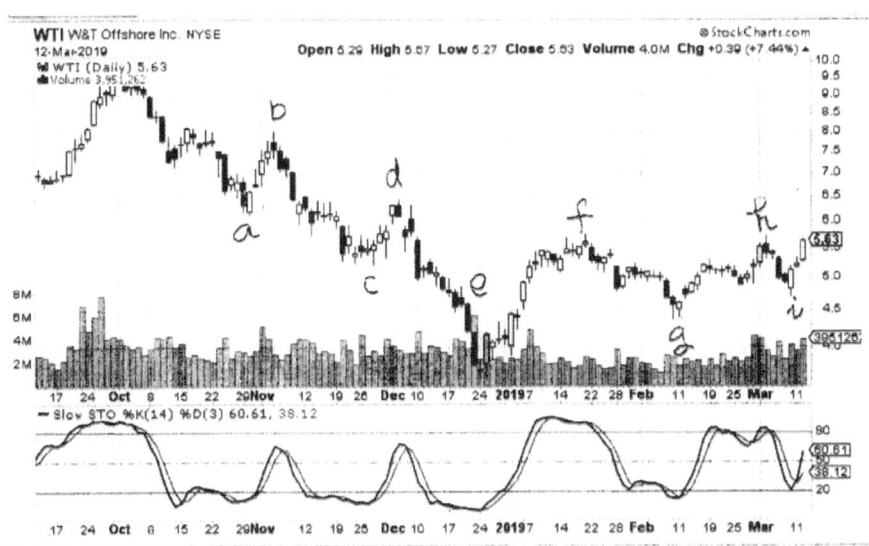

Figure 5.40 Price chart of WTI with hand written annotations

d: This point is in the range of a peak judging from SlowSTO. After a series of ascending bull candles, *d* became a bear candle, which indicated that *d* was a turning day. If selling of a bull fund or buying bear fund was to be done, the best time was before closing of the day.

e: The day was 24 December 2018. This point is after a long and severe descending with bear candles. The candle on this day was extremely short but had a lower wick which did not appear in the past several days. If a bear fund is sold or bull fund is to be purchased, this day was the best. The candle of the next day, 26 December 2018, was a bull candle. A large lower wick indicates that the price went down first after opening, but the price significantly ascended later on this day.

Observation of TVIX price chart in Figure 5.41

Figure 5.41 Price chart of TVIX with hand written annotations

a: Long bull candle with a long upper wick. The long upper wick means that the price ascended once but resisted to go higher and came down. It has a long lower wick, which indicates that there was a strong of selling pressure to lower the price. Next day, the price was significantly lower.

b: A bear candle on the previous day turned to a short bull candle, which indicated that the price movement turned to ascending.

c: Same as *a*.

d: After a series of bear candles the candle on the day was a short bear, but had a long lower wick, which means that the price once went down, resisted to go down further and went up before closing. This reversed the bear movement to the bull movement.

e: The price became higher than the previous day, but the candle was bear and short. It had a long upper wick, which was a scenario of a peak.

f: The opening price was significantly lower than the closing price of the previous day, but price went up before closing making a turning point of price movement.

g: Same as *e*.

h: Relatively short bear candle after a long series of ascending bull candles, but it had a long upper wick, which means that the price went up high but came down, namely the day was a turning point of price movement.

i: The candle is a short bear, but has a long lower wick. Typical candle of a bottom.

j: Although the candle is bull, it had a long upper wick, which indicates that the price went up high once but came down before closing.

k: It is not clear if the day of *k* was the bottom or the day before was the bottom. Once in a while, such an obscure day comes.

l: The candle is short bear with a long upper wick, typical to a peak.

m: A sequence of bear candles changed to a bull candle at *m*.

n: The candle changed to a bull candle from the previous day.

o: Same as *m*

p: The bull candle changed to a bear candle although the closing price is higher than the previous day.

Observation of XTN price chart in Figure 5.42

Figure 5.42 Price chart of XTN with hand written annotations

a: A short bear candle with a long lower wick at a bottom.

b: A clear price reversal happened with a bear candle after a series of ascending bull candles.

c: After a series of bull candles, a peak came with a long upper wick, typical of a peak candle.

d: After a series of bear candles, the reversal of the price movement occurred with a bull candle with a lower wick.

Summary of the observations

Candle patters that appear at the price peaks
- On a peak day, a bull or bear candle with long upper wick tends to appear after a sequence of bull candles
- If a bear candle appears with an opening price higher than the previous day after a sequence of bull candles, it may indicate the peak.

Candle patters that appear at the price bottoms

- On a bottom day, a bull or bear candle with long lower wick tends to appear after a sequence of bear candles
- If a bull candle appears with an opening price lower than the previous day after a sequence of bear candles, it may indicate the bottom.

The method of identifying a peak or bottom explained above may not be perfect, but likelihood of correctness is high if used in parallel with price indicators such as RSI, MACD and SlowSTO.

If a day is judged to be a peak or bottom, trading actions should be done before <u>closing of the day</u>. If the transaction is delayed one day, loss of a few to several percent of the price is likely to occur.

6 Long Term and Short Term Investment in Stocks and ETFs

6.1 High-grade Stocks and Long Term Investment

Apple(AAPL), Amazon(AMZN), Google(GOOGL), Netflix (NFLX), Microsoft(MSFT) are among the high-grade stocks. High-grade stock achieved huge gains in a long term as illustrated next:

```
Google (GOOG)    $1K (2005)  →  $20K (2018)
Apple (AAPL)     $1K (1997)  →  $360K (2018)
Netflix (NFLX)   $1K (2002)  →  $336K (2018)
Amazon (AMZN)    $1K (1994)  →  $276K (2018)
```

The high grade stocks are suitable for long term stock investment, where long term stock investment means that the stocks bought are kept without selling at least for a year. Typically stocks in long term investments are held for many years. Long term investment in high grade stocks have five advantages as follows: (1) the stock price goes up, (2) in downturn of the stock market, loss of the value tend to be minimal, (3) dividends may be earned, (4) lower tax rate for long term investment, and (5) the investor is not required to spend time everyday to watch the market.

If the investor finds one of the next generation super stocks, the gains will be huge and life will be different. Time and effort to find such super stocks is worth and will be well rewarded through the investor's life. The super stocks in the next generation are expected in the area of artificial intelligence, robotics, 5G internet computer industry, particularly high speed computer chips.

Young people are encouraged to buy high grade stocks little by little as they get money to save. The gain is significantly higher than interest of the saving accounts at a bank. Small purchases in every year will accumulate as years pass by, and will reach a huge amount.

For shorter term investments, Figures 6.1-6.5 show price charts for 2.5 years of these stocks. The price of Amazon was tripled, and those of Apple and Google were doubled during the same period.

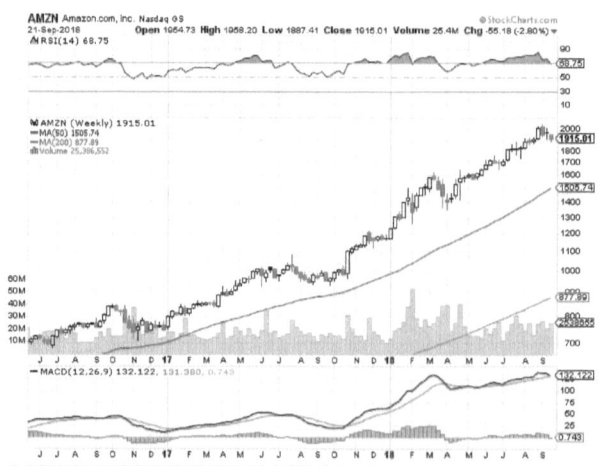

Figure 6.1 2.5 year price history of AMZN (Amazon)

Figure 6.2   2.5 year price history of AAPL (Apple)

Figure 6.3   2.5 year price history of MSFT (Microsoft)

Figure 6.4 2.5 year price history of NFLX (Netflix)

Figure 6.5 2.5 year price history of GOOGL (Google)

Although most of them lost some significant amount of values during the heavy fall between 1 October 2018 to 24 Decmber 2018, the amount of losses were smaller than many other groups of stocks and funds. Nonetheless, such a time is a great opportunity to buy high grade stocks.

Figure 6.6 shows that Amazon lost 28% in the bear market in late 2018.

Figure 6.6 Price chart of Amazon showing the market downturn in late 2018

As shown in Figure 6.7, Google lost 21% from July to the end of December 2018

Figure 6.7 Price chart of Google to the end of December 2018

Figure 6.8 shows that Apple lost about 30% during 3 October 2018 and 3 January 2019.`

Figure 6.8 Apple lost about 30% during 3 October 2018 and 3 January 2019

In case of AAPL shown in Figure 6.8, its stock price started descending together with DOWJ in early October 2018. It lost about 30% by early January 2019, with the largest drop on 3 January 2019. The substantial loss of Apple shown in Figure 6.8 is expected to recover. In case the investor does not want to sell APPL in a downturn of the market, one method of defence against a large loss is to hedge by buying a counter moving fund like TECS or TVIX.

6.2 Technology ETFs

LABU/LABD, UBOT, SOXL/SOXS and TECL/TECS belong to technology 3x ETFs, where the fund names before the "/" sign are bull funds and those after the "/" sign are bear counterparts (bull fund/bear fund). Major movers of the stock marcket are technology stocks, so when DOWJ or SP500 moves significantly, movements of these technology ETFs are large. During the period of early October 2018 to 24 December 2018, LABU, SOXL, and TECL lost, 72%, 57% and 59%, respectively, while DOWJ lost 16%.

Technology stocks and funds move fast in both bear and bull markets. Indeed, when stock market starts declining, the technology stocks and technology bull funds lose values faster than none-tech funds. Also when the stock market recovers from a bottom, technology stocks and technology bull funds go up faster than non-tech funds.

Exactly opposite occurs to the bear technology funds. When a major downturn of stock market starts, the first things you need to do is selling bull funds and buy bear ETFs, particularly bear technology 3x ETFs and TVIX. When the market reaches the bottom, the first thing you need to do is selling bear technology funds and TVIX. As the market ascends just after the bottom, buy bull 3x ETFs particularly in technology .

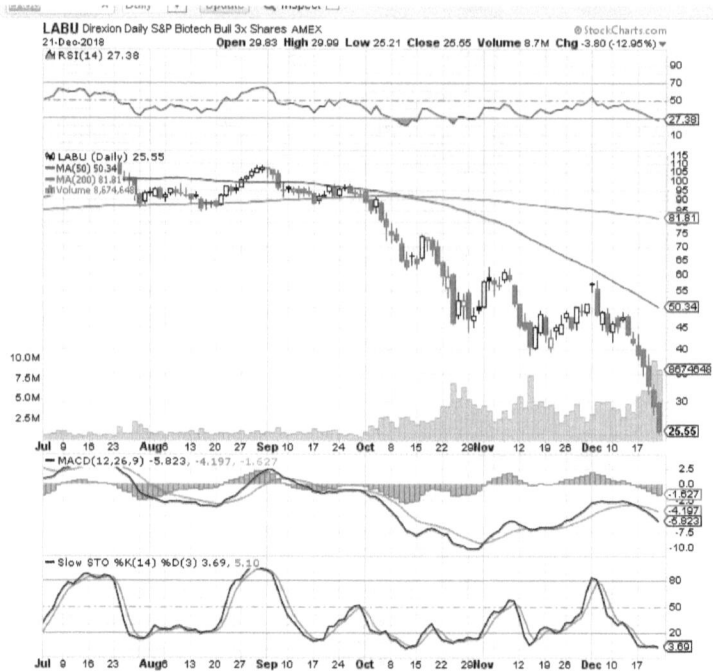

Figure 6.9 Price chart of LABU

Figure 6.10 Price chart of TECL

Figure 6.9 and 6.10 are price charts of LABU and TECL, respectively, which are quite similar to each other. When prices of these ETFs descend, their bear counterparts, LABD and TECS, respectively, should have been held. Entry and exit timing should be found by looking at the price charts of LABD and TECS (see Section 5.14). This is because the price indices such as MACD and SlowSTO do not work well when the price movement downward (or upward) continues for an extended period such as 3 months. For a long descending or ascending, RSI is better than other two indicators.

Referring to Figure 6.9, the price of LABU was $106.7/share on 4 September 2018, and $25.2 on 24 December 2018. In other words, the price of 24 December 2018 was 23.5% of that on 4 September 2018. On the other hand, the price of LABD (the bear counterpart of LABU) was $21.8 and $59.2 respectively on 4 September and 24 December 2018. The price ratio was 2.71, which is equivalent to 171% gain.

The question is how the investor could hold LABD for 4 month period with a confidence. Although the author does not have the price chart of LABD corresponding to Figure 6.9, we can guess how the price indices moved by looking at Figure 6.9, because the graphs of LABD should be nearly inverse for every graph on Figure 6.9. RSI would have come down close to 30 (although not under 30) on 4 september 2018. RSI should have come above 70 about 15 October, when LABD should not have been sold. RSI should have hit 70 two more times, which were also not time to sell. Finally RSI became 70 on 24 December 2018, when LABD should have been sold. None of MACD or SlowSTo were helpful to keep holding LABD until 24 December 2018.

The above observation indicates that finding the timing to sell LABD could not be made using any of the three indices, RSI, MACD and SlowSTO. The only thing that helped keep holding for the four months was if the investor undestood that the market was in a long severe bear market.

In hind sight, there were a number of signs that the market came into a major downturn. First, the market was rising with some acceleration just before the down trend started. A severe downturn often starts while the market is overheated. Once the downturn started, the speed of descending was fast, indicating that the downturn is a major fall. Although the market bounced back a few times, it eventually reached the bottom.

The severeness of the bear market was also observed by looking at price drops of many technology ETS. Therefore, once the down fall started, the invesstor needs to be patient to wait until the down fall finally come to the end.

The statements in the last paragarphs apply to TECL except that the initial date of descending of TECL was about 1 month later than LABU/LABD.

6.3 Crude Oil, Natural GAS and Energy

The price of gasoline we buy at a gas station changes almost every day, but we often see a very low price lasting for one or two weeks. The price of gasoline is based on the price of crude oil, which determines also the prices of oil stocks and ETFs.

UWT, UCO, USOU and GUSH are major bull funds of crude oil, while DWT, SCO, USOD and DRIP are their bear counterparts. WTI is an oil stock.

Figure 6.11 is the price chart of UWT on 18 September 2018.

Figure 6.11 Price chart of UWT (September 18, 2018)

Figure 6.11 shows that there were three times to trade UWT and two trades of DWT following the SlowSTO.

A huge fall of crude oil prices started on October 1, 2018. Figure 6.12 is the price chart of WTI (West Offshore Inc). The price of crude oil on 1 October was about $80/barrel, but came down to $46/barrel on 18 December 2018. In the meantime, WTI was $9.8 on 1 October 2018 but $4.6 on 18 December 2018, which is 47% of the peak on 1 October 2018.

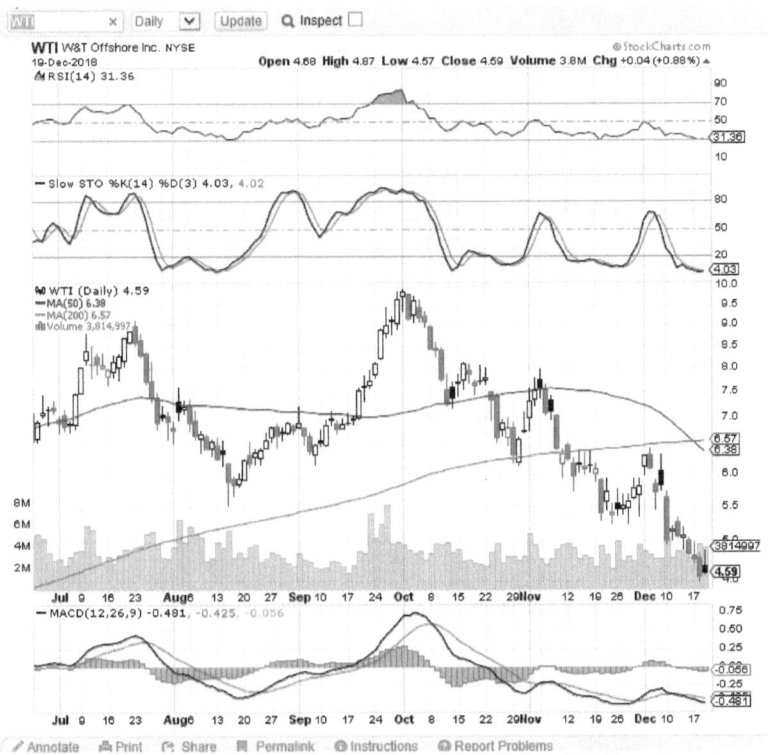

Figure 6.12 Price chart of WTI (December 19, 2018)

The falls of 3x crude oil ETFs, namely UWT, USOU, UCO, during the same period were far more spectacular.

As Figure 6.13 shows, the price of UWT reached a peak on 1 October 2018 but started descending and continued its descending until the end of 2018. During this period, the peak price was $47.4 and the bottom price was $8.2. That is the bottom price was 17.3% of the peak price. The prices of USOU and UCO fell similarly, as Figure 6.14 illustrate.

**Figure 6.13 Price chart of UWT
(14 September 2018 through March 1 2019)**

Figure 6.14   Price chart of USOU (4 January 2019)

When bull oil ETF falls, their bear counterparts, namely DWT, USOD, or/and SCO, shown in Figures 6.15, 6.16 and 6.17, are the ETFs to make money. If bought on 1 October 2018, the value of each ETF at their bottom on 24 December 2018 were 3.8 fold for DWT, 3 fold for USOD, and 2.5 fold for SCO

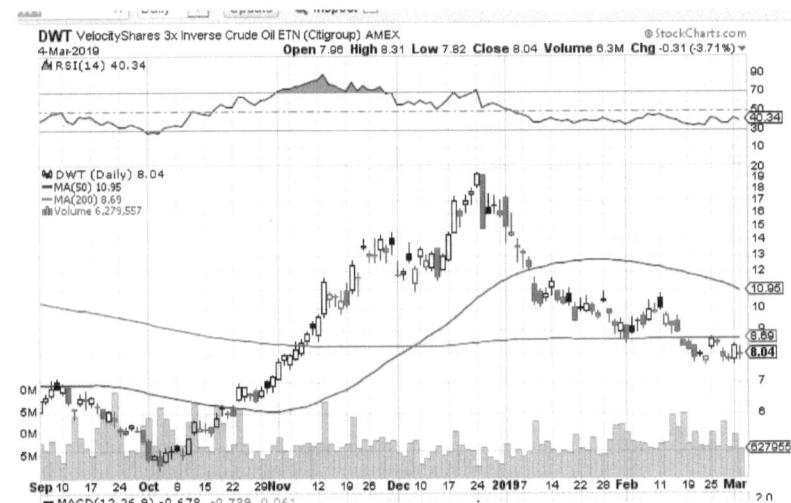

Figure 6.15 Price chart of DWT (4 March 2019)

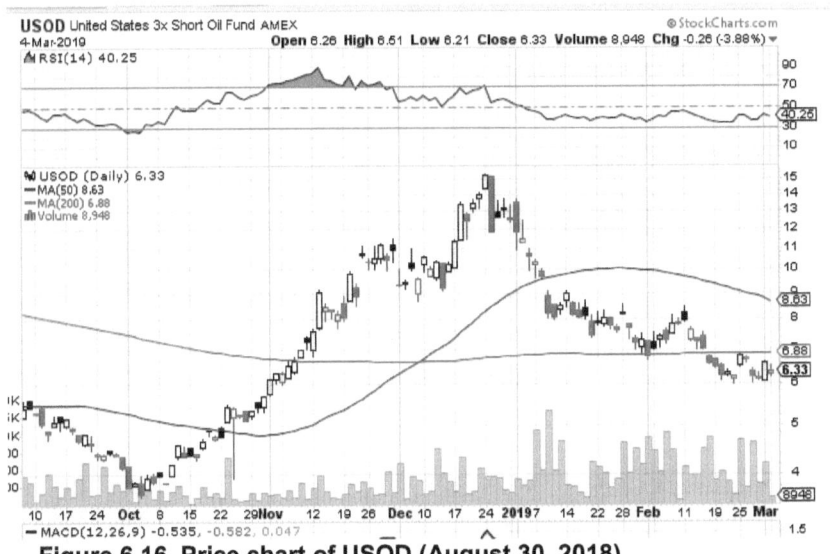

Figure 6.16 Price chart of USOD (August 30, 2018)

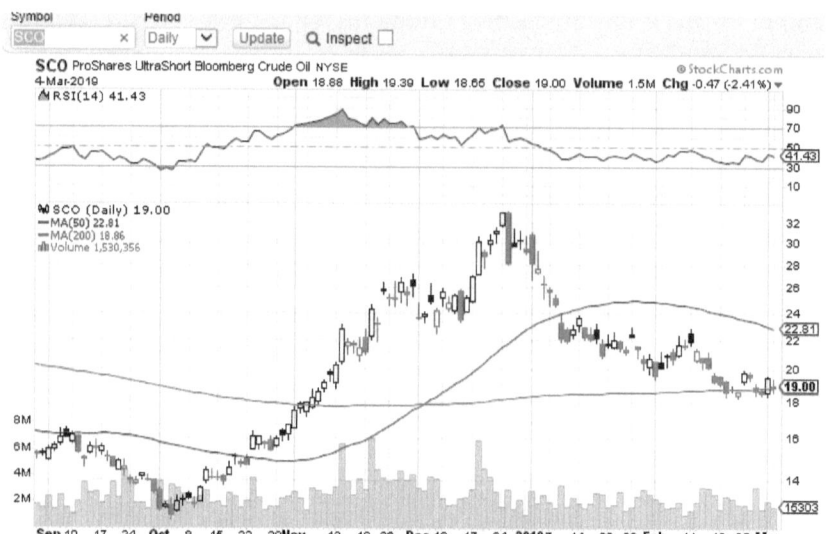
Figure 6.17 Price chart of SCO (4 March 2019)

After the bottom on 24 December 2018, all of the bull oil ETF started rising as seen in Figure 6.13. The price of UWT on 24 December 2018 was $8.22, while that on 1 February 2019 was 14.94. The gain factor was 14.94/8.22 = 1.82, or the gain in about one month was 82%.

Although we did not mention earlier in this section, there are more crude oil and natural gas funds including GASL and ERX. GASX and ERY are bear counterparts of GASL and ERX, respectively.

6.4 Foreign Investment Funds

There are many funds for foreign investment. Here we look at BRZU (Brazil 3x bull), YNN (China bull), KORU (Korea 3x bull), RUSS/RUSL (Russia bull/bear), JPNL (Japan 3x bull), INDL (India 3x bull) and MEXX (Mexico 3x bull).

BRZU (Brazil bull 3x fund)

BRZU is a 3x bull ETF of Brazil investment. Figure 6.18 is a price chart of BRZU. There is no bear counterpart, so short selling is needed to invest when the price descends.

Figur 6.18   Price chart of BRZU on 31 Aug 2018

The gain in ascending from the end of June to the beginning of August was 60%, and the gain in descending from August 2 to September 16 was 80% (if short selling was done), so the gain factor for the entire cycle from the bottom to the next bottom was 1.6 x 1.8 = 2.9 or 190% gain. In other words, the total investment money would have been almost trippled.

The next cycle of ascending started on September 16 and seems to have reversed on October 8, during which the gain factor wass about 1.9. If descending has started, it is expected to come down to about $15/share. If so, an expected gain will be 1.56. That is, the total gain factor will be 1.9 x 1.56 = 2.9, namely the total money will be come 2.9 times in one cycle, which is in less than 2 months.

The price movement of BRZU is often violent. Recently the price jumped 20% in a day. Although the price movements are bumpy, the gains from a bottom to the next peak, and from a peak to the next bottom by means of short selling, tend to be very high.

YINN (China 3x bull)

The price movement of YINN may look chaotic, but a closer look at reveals that YINN's price movement has a repeated pattern with an oscillation of wave length about 2 to 4 weeks long.

Figure 6.19 Price chart of YINN on 6 Sep 2018

Figure 6.20 Price chart of YINN on 5 Oct 2018

Figure 6.21 Price chart of YINN on 8 March 2019

Figure 6.21 indicates that MACD well renders the buy and sell timings

KORU (Korea 3x bull)

Figure 6.22 Price chart of KORU on 19 Dec 2018

The Korean economy is currently in turmoil due to the governmental and economic frictions between Korea and Japan as well as Korea and China. But, such affairs do not matter to us because our interest is in if the fund price widely moves up and down.

RUSL (Russia bull 3x)

Figure 6.23   Price chart of RUSS on 19 Dec 2018

Russian economy is heavily dependent on its crude oil production. Because the crude oil price descended since 1 October 2018, RUSL declined along with the crude oil price. Interestingly, RUSL is significantly affected by US stock market. RUSS is the bear counterpart of RUSL

JPNL (Japan bull 3x)

Japan has strong technology and economy. For a long term investment, that is a good thing. For short investment, we have to watch how JPNL moves well for us. See Figures 6.24 and 6.25 for price movements of JPNL.

Figure 6.24   Price chart of JPNL (5 October 2018)

Figure 6.25   Price chart of JPNL (8 March 2019)

INDL (India bull 3x)

On 5 October 2018, INDL was falling fast to a bottom as seen in Figure 6.26. If INDL had been sold short on 27 August 2018, the gain on 5 October 2018 would have been 84%. As of 5 Oct 2018, we could not see how far it would fall further, but RSI was already below 30%, and SlowSTO was not only below 20 but it was 1.72. The price is expected to go up violently after the coming bottom. Therefore, INDL was an excellent candidate for purchase as of October 5.

Figure 6.26 Price chart of INDL on 5 October 2018

A verdict for this prediction is seen in the Figure 6.27.

Figure 6.27 Price chart of INDL on 8 March 2019

If INDL was bought on 8 October 2018, however, the investor must have a painful time as it entered another downturn about one week later. If INDL was quickly sold as a peak was reached on 16 October, it could have been bought again on 28 October 2018 by following SlowSTO (not shown here) passing 20 from below.

MEXX (Mexico bull 3x)

From middle of April to early June 2018, there was a big falling, in which the gain could have been 70% if sold short (see Figure 6.28). Then, ascending from the first week to the end of July could have gained 54%. From early August, MEXX entered an oscillating mode. The height of the waves were about 10%. This is not much, but the total gain from a bottom to the next bottom is about 20% within a month.

MEXX got into a big fall starting on 10 October 2018, which ended on 26 November 2018 as seen in Figure 6.29. During the entire October and most of November 2018, SlowSTO was almost continuously under 20. The bottom was on 26 November 2018. There were quick formation of bottom and peak between 29 October and 10 November. If the investor sold MEXX short earlier, the investor should have ignored this pair of bottom and peak because the market was in a strong descending mode, or might have passes through by quick tradings.

Figure 6.28 Price chart of MEXX, April 2018 to October 2018

Figure 6.29 Price chart of MEXX, October 2018 to 8 March 2019

6.5 Volatility Index Funds and SP 500 Bull/Bear 3x Funds

SPXL is a 3x bull ETF that moves along with SP500 index, while SPXS is its bear counterpart.

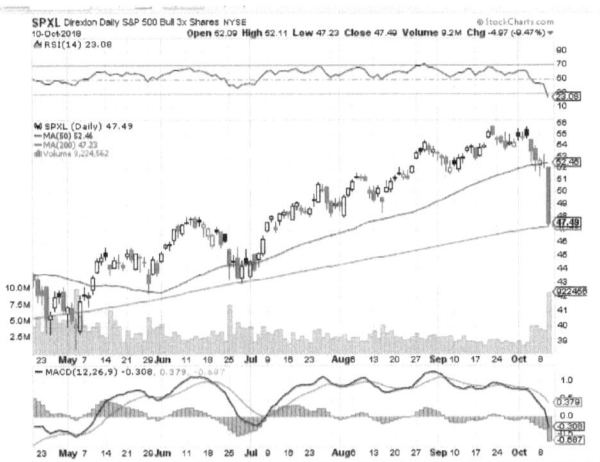

Figure 6.30 Price chart of SPXL, S&P bull 3x fund

Figure 6.31 Price chart of SPXS, S&P 3x bear fund

Volatility ETFs are associated with SP500 index and popular among short term investors. Their prices go up when SP500 does down. These ETFs are tied to CBOE Volatility Index (VIX), which represents the price volatility in the option prices of the S&P 500 Index for 30 days in the future.

There are 15 volatility ETFs as follows[5]: VXX, UVXY, TVIX, SVXY, VIXY, ZIV, VXXB, VIXM, VXZ, VIIX, EXIV, XVZ, VXZB, VMIN, EVIX. Two price charts of TVIX are shown in the following two figures.

---

[5] https://www.etf.com/channels/volatility-etfs

Figure 6.32 Price chart of TVIX, volatility index 2x ETN (April to October 2018)

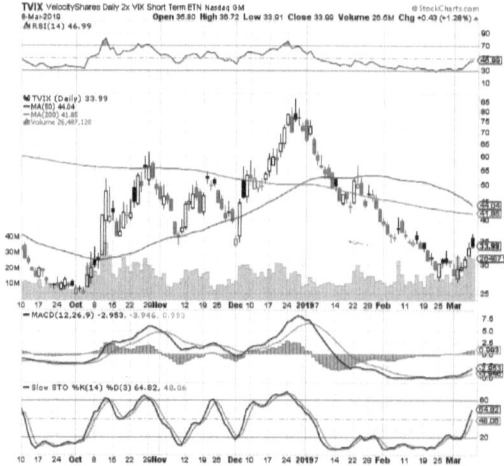

Figure 6.33 Price chart of TVIX, volatility index 2x ETN (September 2018 to 8 March 2019)

Figures 6.32 and 6.33 show that the timings of buying TVIX are well rendered as SlowSTO ascended from below 20 and passes the line of 20. Selling timings are also well indicated by the peaks of SlowSTO when is passes 80. When the stock market is bear and volatile, trading TVIX alone can make a large sum of gains. Indeed, if TVIX is bought on 1 October 2018 and sold on 24 December, the gain was 220%.

There are some other uses of TVIX, too. That is, TVIX moves in the opposite direction of SP500 (or DOWJ), while TECL moves closely with SP500 (or DOWJ). Therefore, the timings of selling TECL at its peak coincide exactly with the timings of buying TVIX, and the timings of buying TECL are same as the timing of the selling TVIX.

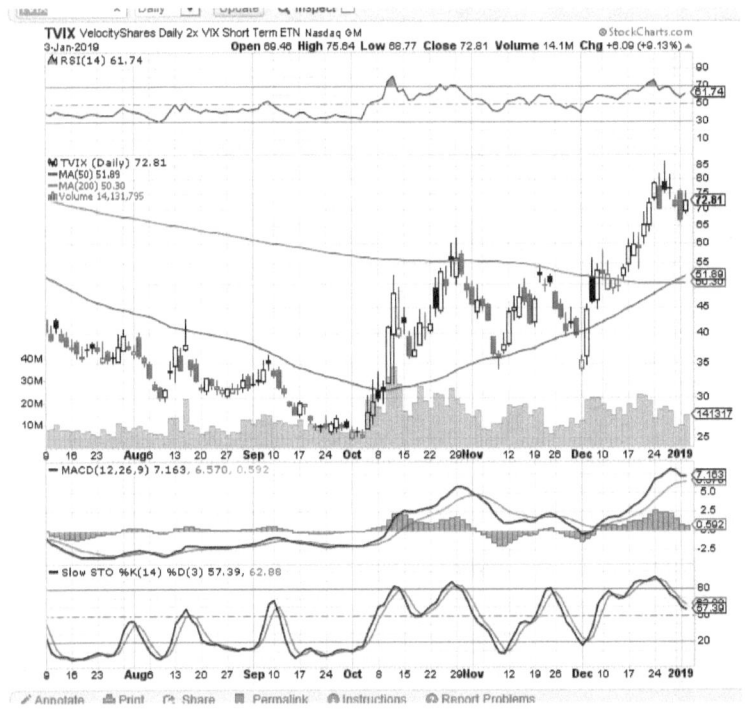

Figure 6.34 Price chart of TVIX (9 July 2018 to 3 January 2019)

One nature that investors should be aware is that the amount of price changes of TVIX is greatly affected by not only by the amount but the speed of price change of SP500. In other words, if the change of SP500 is fast, TVIX ascends fast, but if the change of SP500 is slow despite the amount of change is the same, the change of TVIX is smaller.

Figure 6.35 Price chart of TECL (9 July 2018 to 3 January 2019)

Knowing the existence of the inverse relation between TVIX and TECL, an investment strategy may be developed such that the stock investment money is used almost always in either of TVIX or TECL, both of which are among the highest performer in making money.

Understanding that the peaks and bottoms of TVIX coincide with bottoms and peaks, respectively, of TECL, the decision making of buying and selling timing of TECL may be done using the price chart TVIX. The peaks and bottoms of TVIX are often clearer on the price charts than those of TECL, because the wick of the candles at peaks and bottom of TVIS tend to be longer than TECL. Therefore, the price movement direction is easier to find on the TVIX price chart than on the price chart of TECL. The same principle applies to other bull technical funds which move in tandem with SP500 or DOWJ.

6.6 Penny Stocks and Marijuana Stocks

Penny stocks refer to the stocks under $1 per share. There are countless penny stocks. Penny stocks can be lucrative if you can find good ones, which is not easy because there are zillions of penny stocks.

One characteristic feature of penny stocks is that the price tend to explode violently pushing up the price to a multiple of the price before the explosion.

One group of active penny stocks at this time is in the marijuana industry. Presently marijuana is legalized in increasing number of states in US and other countries. Marijuana also became legal in Canada in October 2018. A large number of companies which produce marijuana products have emerged in U.S. and Canada. Most of the stocks of these companies started as penny stocks. A few examples of price movements are shown in the following figures.

ATTBF

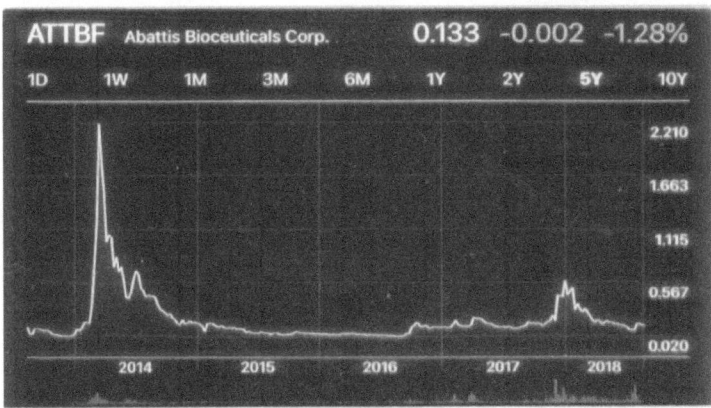

Figure 6.36 Five year chart of ATTBF

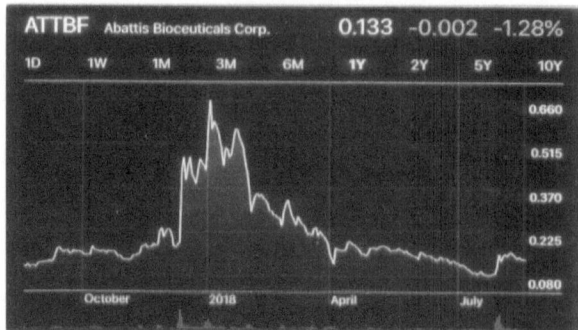

Figure 6.37 One year chart of ATTBF

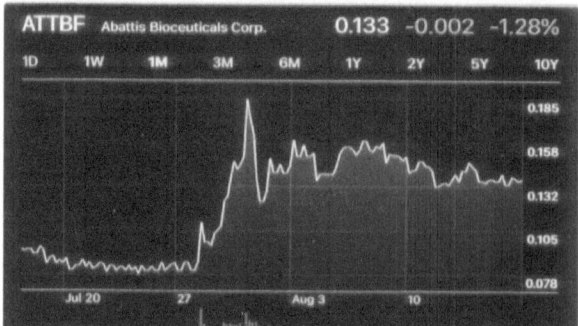

Figure 6.38 Two month chart of ATTBF

The price of ATTBF jumped with a gain factor of 10 from 2016 to 2017. Also from the middle to 2017 to the beginning of 2018, the price increased by a factor of 4 (see Figure 6.37). After that, the price descended once, but then it ascended by a factor of 2 (see Figure 6.38).

MCOA

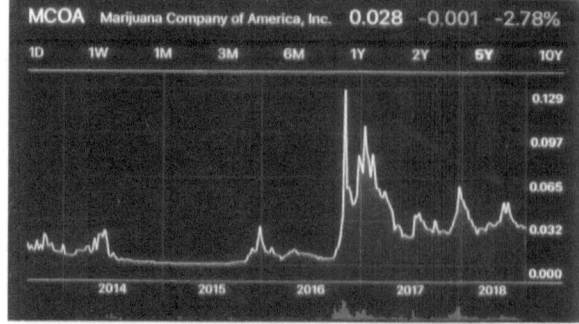

Figure 6.39 5 year price history of MCOA

MCOA erupted suddenly after a long dormant period with a violent uprising of the price (see Figure 6.39), which often subsided and returned to the original or a little higher price. The chart of price (Figure 6.39) looks like a fractal, perhaps because the investor's actions during the eruption are similar each time. If each eruption can be detected early and can be bought just before each eruption, a large gain can be obtained.

When investing in penny stocks, the most important task is to watch many penny stocks, and trade cautiously when a good chance is found.

There are a few companies who do this job for investors. If a contract is made with one of the companies, they will send text or phone message when a chance arrives. However, a large number of their clients receive the same message, and start buying such a penny stick, which quickly increases the price. So when you try to buy the stock, the price may be already high. Also if you are employed, stopping your work and spending time to buy/sell stock shares may not be possible.

An ideal way is to develop a unique, one-of-a-kind computer program that constantly surveys the prices of a huge number of penny stocks and report only to you of good opportunities.

On the other hand, investing in penny stock in long term stock investment may not be a bad idea. If good penny stocks are identified, their stocks may be bought as a long term investment. Remember, many of currently good stocks started as a penny stock.

6.7 Bitcoin

Bitcoin's current price and historical chart can be seen as bitcoin index, $NYXBT. An example is shown in the following figure.

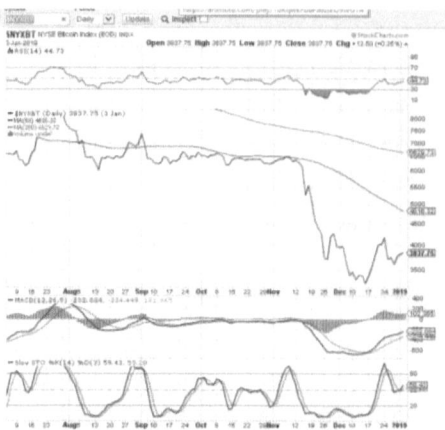

Figure 6.40 Chart of Bitcoin Index $NYXBT

To trade bitcoin for investment, it is not necessary to buy and sell bitcoin. A much easier way is to trade a fund named, GBTC, which moves proportionally to the price of bitcoin. The price of a share is nearly a 10th of the actual bitcoin, and can be traded like a stock.

A long history of the price of bitcoin is shown in Figure 6.41. The price behavior of bitcoin is similar to a bubble of the marijuana stocks or silver price[6]. Ascending of bitcoin price between January 2016 and December 2017 was spectacular. Indeed, the price was $308 in January 2016, $891 in January 2017, and $19,280 in December 2017. The price on 5 September 2018 was $6,944.

Figure 6.41 History of bitcoin price

---

[6]More details of silver price history are written in the next section.

The price movement of GBTC are shown in the following two figures.

Figure 6.42 Price chart of BGTC from July 2017 to October 2018

Figure 6.43 Price chart of GBTC from mid-July to 4 Jan 2019

Although the bitcoin price has been descending since the end of 2017, it still moves up occasionally. GBTC has no counterpart of bear version. Short selling of GBTC may not be easy at an ordinary stock brokerage but is possible at Ally Invest[7].

There is good chance in the future that bitcoin may goes up extremely high again. That is when some major monetary system, including Chinese Yuan, European Euro, US Dollar, Japanese Yen, is significantly disturbed.

---

[7] https://secure.ally.com/

6.8 Gold and Silver

Gold and silver investment may be done by either buying actual metals or buying stocks of mining companies. Investment into gold and silver is not difficult, and it can be very lucrative. Gold and silver shine particularly when stock market goes down severely. When gold price outbreaks, price of gold mining funds ascends very rapidly, giving us great opportunities to earn serious amount of money.

Buying metals is suitable if preservation of the value is the objective. On the other hand, if earning money quickly is the objective, buying funds of gold/silver mining companies can be by far more lucrative and easier. However, if you hold gold/silver mining funds for a long time with little movement of gold price, you will lose money because of the cost of the funds[8].

Figure 6.44-A History of gold in 18 years

---

[8] There is a cost of operating a fund. The higher is the leverage, the higher is the cost. The cost is included in the price of the fund. For example, even if the average price of the stocks in the fund is unchanged, the price of the fund goes down day by day because of the cost of operation. This is why highly leveraged funds are not suitable for long term investment.

Figure 6.44-B   History of gold in 5 years

Let us now look at long term and short term histories of gold price. Figure 6.44-A is a gold price history since 1974. More recent history is shown in Figure 6.44-B.

Notice in both figures that top of most peaks is very sharp. It means that the direction of the price reverses very fast when a peak is reached. The same is true to the bottoms, too. Observe also that the highest peaks are double-, triple- or multiple-peaked. This is typical in bubbles. The first peak is formed because, as the price goes very high, profit takers start selling at some point, which put pressure on the price and eventually the price starts descending. As the price becomes lower, profit taking slows down but also late comers start buying, which drives the price upward again forming the second peak. After the second peak, the price continues to come down for some time, and so on.

Trading bull gold ETFs such as JNUG and NUGT while the gold price goes up (and selling near the peak) is extremely lucrative. The latest super peaks of gold ETF occurred in 2016 as seen in Figure 6.44-C. The price of JNUG was $10.60/share on 8 March 2019, but was $123 at the peak in 2016.

This high ratio of the peak price to the bottom price of JNUG, namely 123/10.6=11.6, was unique in 2016. This was not caused by a very high peak price of gold in 2016 but rather the low price of gold in late 2015 to very early 2016, plus extreme enthusiasm in Gold miners ETFs. This high ratio of the peak to bottom is therefore a rare incidence, but we do not need such an extreme incidence to make money with gold ETFs.

Figure 6.44-C Price history of JNUG in 5 years

87

https://www.marketwatch.com/investing/fund/jnug

After the highest peaks have become a history, the gold price tends to oscillate. There are great opportunities in the period of oscillations. Gold mining funds oscillate more significantly than the price of gold, so buying and selling bull and bear gold mining funds alternatively could still make awesome profits. For us investors, it is important to have enough knowledge on how to trade in an extreme circumstance as well as in usual market.

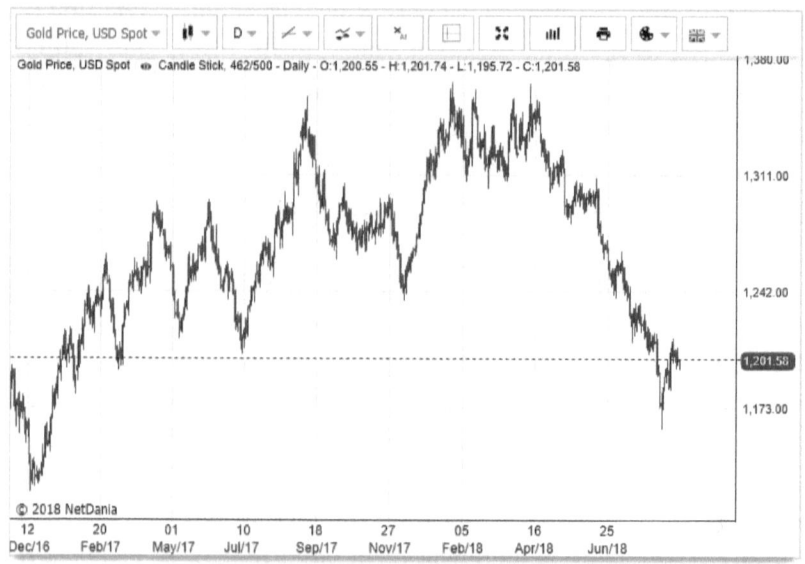

Figure 6.45 Change of 1 ounce gold price for 1 and half year
https://goldprice.org/live-gold-price.html

The price history of silver since 1998 is shown in Figure 6.46.

Figure 6.46　History of 1 ounce silver

Figure 6.46 is a silver price history since 1998. Silver price reached $48/ounce in April 2011, but came down to $14 in November 2015. It bounced back to $20 in June 2016. After then it continued to descend to $14. Figure 6.47 is a more recent history of silver price.

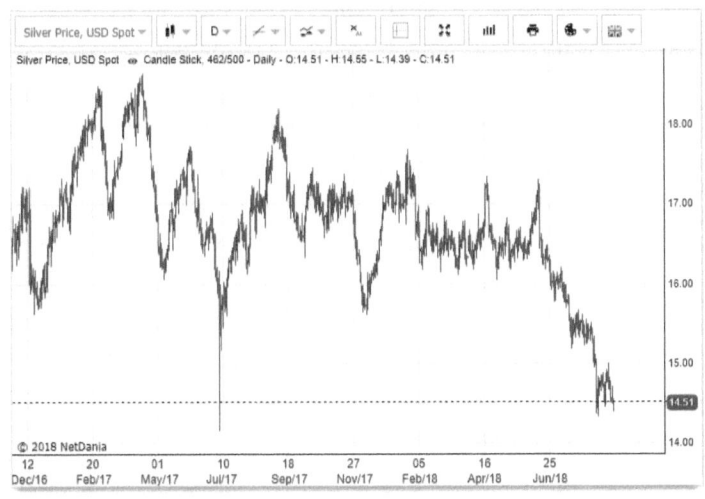

Figure 6.47　Change of 1 ounce silver price for 1 and half year
https://goldprice.org/live-gold-price.html

Coming back to the subject of gold price, Figure 6.48 is very interesting and educational as well. It shows that since 1900, there were three periods when DOWJ outperformed. But gold outperformance always came while DOWJ declined significantly.

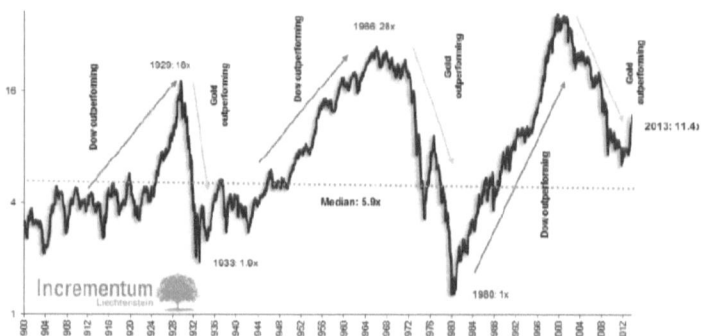

Figure 6.48 Alternating outperformance between Gold price and DOWJ
https://seekingalpha.com/instablog/428250-michael-clark/4885515-gold-cycle-gold-good-2019-historical-study-gold-prices-conclusion

So when gold will outperform next time? The answer is when the current stock market goes into a super recession. The bottom of December 2018 was not deep enough to cause a sharp rise of gold price, because the economy was still booming, the unemployment rate was low. It is the opinion of many analysts that the downturn of December 2018 was mainly due to uncertainty caused by foreign trade frictions. Economy may still be booming for another year, while corporate earning may rise in 2019 because of the corporate tax cut.

The prices of gold mining stocks move in close tie with the gold price. They are not proportional because there is no profit for the gold mining companies if the gold price is the same as the gold production cost or lower. Indeed, the prices of gold mining companies are proportional to the profits of the gold mining companies. The gold production cost varies among different gold mining companies, but roughly speaking it is somewhere between $600 and $800/ounce currently, while the gold price is $1299 to $1300 per ounce.

Recent price history of gold can be seen also by a chart of the gold index, $GOLD, as illustrated in Figure 6.49.

The fund named GLD mimics the price of physical gold, which can be traded through a stock brokerage. Buying GLD has the same effect as buying gold except there are no needs to transport and storage physical gold. Also, there is no price markup by the gold dealers.

Figure 6.49 Gold price index, $GOLD

There are many stocks of mining companies as well as ETFs/ETNs, some of which are listed in Table 6.1.

Table 6.1 Major gold stocks and funds

Gold mining stocks	Gold ETFs/ETNs
ABX: Barrick Cold	GDXJ
HL: Hecla mining	GDX
CDE: Coeur mining	NUGT gold mining 3x bull
RGLD: Royal Gold	DUST gold mining 3x bear
OCANF: Oceans Gold	JNUG junior gold mining 3x bull
NG: Nova Gold	JDST junior gold mining 3x bear
FCX: Freeport-McMoRan	USL silver mining 3x bull
GORO: Gild Resources	DSLV silver mining 3x bear
NEM: Neumont Mining	GLD
ALIAF: Alcer Gold	

For short term investments, 3x bull and 3x bear funds in Table 6.1 are most profitable if used successfully.

$HUI[9] is an index to show performance of gold mining companies as illustrated in Figure 6.50.

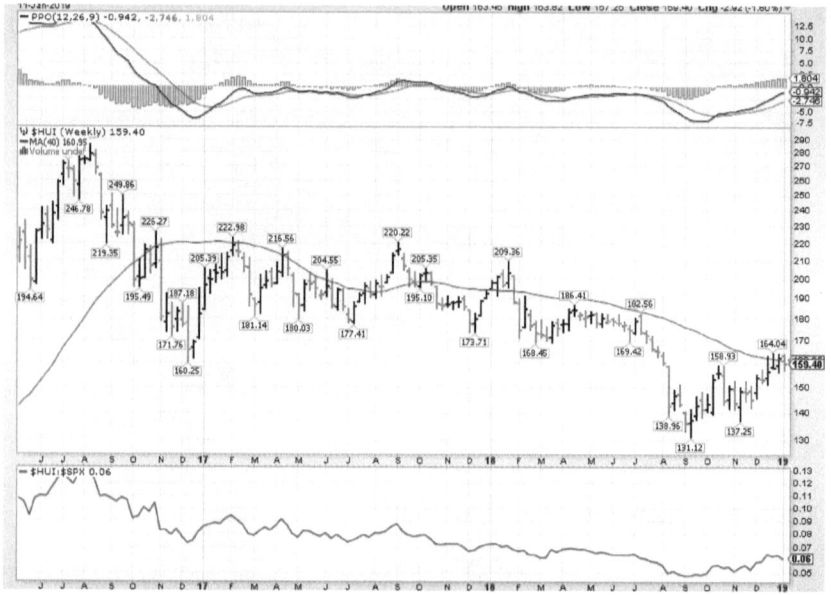

Figure 6.50 Chart of $HUI

Stock prices of silver mining companies are different from gold mining companies, yet they move in close relation with the gold mining companies. That means, when the gold prices move up or down, the silver mining companies move up or down mostly together.

---

[9] $HUI is abbreviation of NYSE Arca Gold BUGS Index, called simply HUI Index, which a modified equal dollar weighted index of companies involved in gold mining. The HUI Index was developed with a base value of 200.00 as of March 15, 1996. The HUI Index currently consists of 15 of the largest and most widely held public gold production companies. A chart of HUI can be obtained with stockahrts.com by typing $HUI in the window of symbol.

Figure 6.51 Price chart of JNUG (August 16, 2018)

In investing gold mining funds, predicting the direction of the price movement of the fund is some times difficult. Referring to Figure 6.51, the period between May to 17 August, 2018, was a precarious time for the gold investors. Many gold investors subscribe to one or more of the gold investment advisory newsletters[10]. During this period, at least a couple of advisors assured that investors should stay in bull because the gold price historically goes up in September and October. Many investors believed the advisors. When they saw a small surge in early July, they thought it was the beginning of a serious ascending and bought bull 3x ETFs. They even thought that a small dip of the price on July 22 as a bottom because they believed what the advisors wrote. After this, however, the descending movement of gold mining stocks and funds accelerated and finally reached a deep bottom on 16 August 2018. They lost much money.

---

[10] An example is Goldpredict.com News Letter Sample: Includes outlook of 2019 stock market
https://goldpredict.com/archives/17128

How could this be prevented? The answer was in checking with SlowSTO of gold miners fund like JNUG. See Figure 6.52. A very clear peak of SlowSTO touching 80 appeared on July 9, as seen in the left edge of Figure 6.52. The peak can also be seen in Figure 6.51. If the gold investors noticed it rather than blindly believing the advisors, not only such a huge loss could have been prevented, but also made a substantial amount of money.

Figure 6.52 JNUG price movement with SlowSTO

That means, as seen in Figure 6.53, if JDST was bought when its price was $46 on July 9, 2018, the price went up to $88.6 on 16 August 16, 2018, that is a 92% gain.

Notice in Figure 6.52, a divergence between price chart and MACD appeared between 20 August and 22 October 2018. Also, SlowSTO came down to below 20 on 16 July, it was not a sign to buy because SlowSTO stayed below 20 until 27 August 2018. This is an example of not to buy even when SlowSTO moves to below 20.

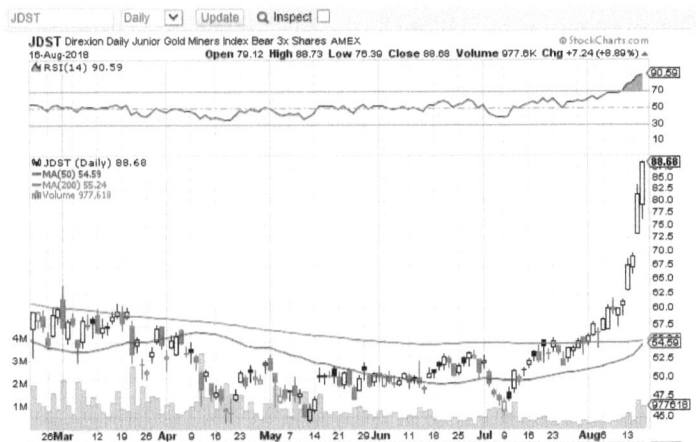

Figure 6.53 JDST price movement before August 17

On 2 September 2018, one of the advisors admitted his error, and wrote in his news letter the following remarks (abridged):

"I thought that 2018 is a year of rising gold price. There is still its possibility left, but by now the possibility has diminished significantly. Then, what is happening? The gold price is affected by interest rate, prospect of inflation, government fiscal policy, demand for gold investment and consumer sentiment, among others. Presently in US, the financial institutions are prioritizing stock investment to gold investment. In fact, the gold market cannot compete with technology stocks.

This can be said to be the Trump effect. In 2016, the economy was heading to recession, and gold price was surging. The gold price that was down to $1045(/ounce) rose to $1377 in June 2016. However, everything changed when Trump became the president. Economy turned to go upward, the new tax policy invigorated the business cycle. If Hilary Clinton was elected, the gold price would have been rising upward.

This does not mean the opportunities of gold was lost. Rather, Trump presidency delayed such opportunities a year or two. The business cycle has come close to a peak, the growth momentum has exhausted, and the curve of profits is turning downward. The US economy is expected to turn to negative. The slowing down of profits is a precursor of recession.

Gold price is supported by ICS (Index of Consumer Sentiment)[11]. There is almost no consumers who think of gold, because the incomes of people have been rising, inflation is mild, and jobless rate is at the lowest level in the several years of the past.

President Trump did well to raise stock price but brought difficulties to the gold investors. For the gold price to go up, something like dismay of economy, political disorder, or severe geopolitical crisis will be necessary. If people become aware of the down turn of economy, their interest in gold will increase. There is sign that President Trump can be pulled down from his position. The gold price will soar if that happens.

There is not much we can do now except watching the low prices of the gold mining stocks. In the meantime, we should to pay our attention to other opportunities such as bitcoin and crude oil."

---

[11] ICS: Index of Consumer Centiment. In 2011, ICS came a bottom at 55, and the gold price peaked at $1923. Since then ICS continued to rise until 2016, then it descended and the gold price went up to $1377. Currently it is around 96. If it comes down to 86 in the future, it will be a good environment for gold to a higher price than now.

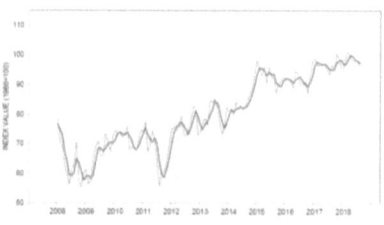

Figure F1 US Consumer Price Index

Figure 6.54 Possible trade of JNUG after 17 August 2018

Trading JNUG after August 16 was by no means easy. First, there was fear, and second, the direction of the price movement after August 16 was hard to predict. However, with the aide of RSI, MACD and SlowSTO, multiple tradings as indicated in Figure 6.54 by hand written arrow signs could have been made, where black (or ascending) arrows indicate the periods to own JNUG, and red (or descending) arrows are the periods to own JDST. During this period, DOWJ descended severely, that might have distracted the attention of the investors, making focusing on gold mining funds difficult.

Another thing to observe in Figure 6.54 is that if MACD is fully respected, successful trades could have been achieved as follows. Buy JDST on 9 July, sell JDST on 20 August and buy JNUG, sell JNUG on 15 October and buy JDST, sell JDST on 13 October, and buy JNUG at the same time, and keep it until the next bottom on 24 December 2018.

Figure 6.55 Price chart of JNUG up to January 2019

Figure 6.56 is the price chart of JNUG for 10 September 2018 through 6 March 2019.

Figure 6.56 Price cart of JNUG between 10 September 2018

through 6 March 2019

Figure 6.55 indicates that trading of JNUG during this period was not as hard as in the period before 20 August 2018.

7 Relations between DOWJ and Stocks/ETFs

Many stocks move in tandem with SP500 and DOWJ. In fact, peaks and bottoms of those stocks and ETFs occur concurrently with peaks and bottoms of SP500 and DOWJ. This fact guides us to find buying and selling timings by watching the peaks and bottoms of SP500 or DOWJ.

Also as mentioned in Section 6.5, peaks and bottoms of TVIX coincide well with the bottoms and peaks, respectively, of SP500 and DOWJ. Identifying those on the price charts of TVIX by watching the shapes of candles may be easier than on the price charts of SP500 or DOWJ or bull funds.

7.1 Substantial Losses in Downturn of Stock Market

In late 2018, DOWJ and SP500 experienced large losses. When DOWJ and SP500 suffer large losses, many stocks and funds go down together. We first show price charts of DOWJ and SPXL before 17 October 2018 in Figures 7.1 and 7.2.

Figure 7.1 Chart of DOWJ index (15 October 2018)

Figure 7.2 Chart of SPXL (15 October 2018)

The following figures show price charts of several funds that descended with DOWJ.

Figure 7.3 Chart of SOXL (15 October 2018)

Figure 7.4 Chart of TECL (15 October 2018)

Figure 7.5 Chart of LABU (15 October 2018)

Figure 7.6   Chart of UBOT (15 October 2018)

Figure 7.7   Chart of INDL (15 October 2018)

Figure 7.8   Chart of KORU (15 October 2018)

Among the stocks and funds that descended with DOWJ and SPX, the technical stocks suffered most severely.

Most of the investors hate big downturn of the stock market, but downturns are real opportunities if you know how to trade in the bear market. In 2019, very harsh bear markets may occur more than once. In fact, each of the US/China trade war, Russian Gate, possible Brexit without agreement and failure of Deutsche Bank may cause very severe bear stock market not only in US but worldwide.

It is believed that only 5% of stock investors are familiar with trading bear funds. The readers of this book should practice trading bear funds or short selling when the stock market nosedives.

7.2 Early Detection of a Downturn

In a bull market like the whole year of 2017, investors forget that a bear market may come any time. A sudden descending of stock prices that started in October 2018 was a big surprise. If such a severe downturn is detected early, we can prepare for the opportunities during the bear markets.

The first way of detection is to watch the movements of small cap funds such as TNA. Figures 7.9 and 7.10 show weekly charts of DOWJ and TNA, respectively. Both are similar, but we compare the movements of both at peaks in January 2018 and October 2018. The price movements of DOWJ toward the peak of January 2018 looks like exponential, while the speed of ascending of TNA was slowing down. In the next case of the DOWJ peak of October 2018, ascending of DOWJ continued through September but TNA started descending in September, which is one month earlier. These comparisons indicate that downturn of DOWJ can be detected by comparing DOWJ to TNA particularly when DOWJ ascends fast.

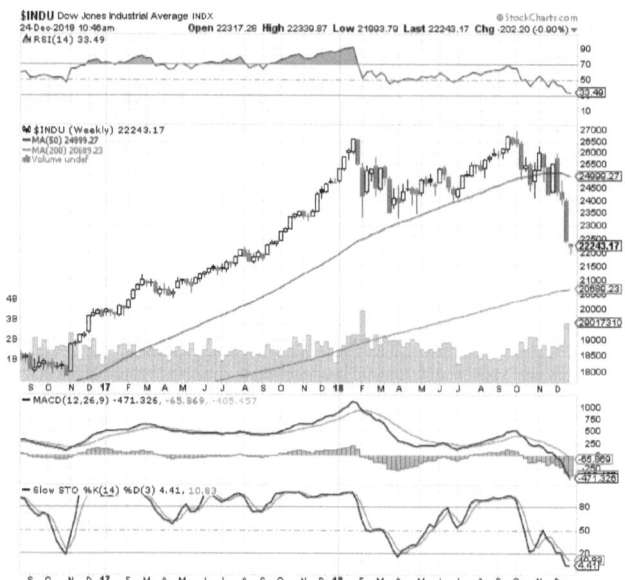

Figure 7.9   Weekly pirce chart of DOWJ (December 24, 2018)

Figure 7.10   Weekly price chart of TNA (Small cap bull 3x, December 24, 2018)

A bear counterpart of TNA is TZA, which may be used also to predict the near future of DOWJ. Even a large amount of money can be earned by buying TZA during a downturn of the stock market.

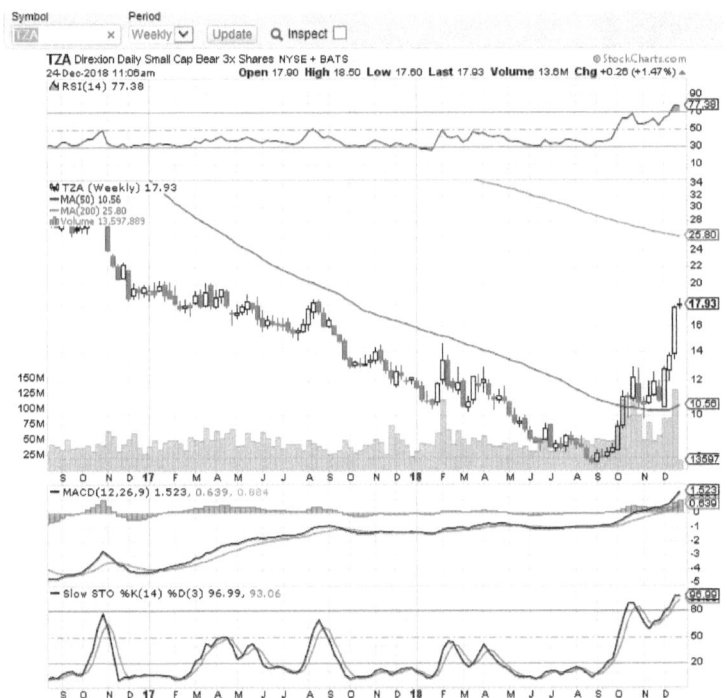

Figure 7.11   Weekly price chart of TZA (Small cap bull 3x, December 24, 2018))

Indeed, at the bottom of TZA on 31 August, the price of TZA was $7.85, which became $17.7 (2.25-fold or 125% gain) on 24 December 2018. Look at the RSI and SlowSTO on 24 December 2018. They are above 70 and 80 respectively on 24 October 2018, indicating they were at a peak and will soon come down. Again, it means that DOWJ would start ascending in near future. The author is writing this paragraph on December 24, 2018. See the verdict to this predication in January 2019. (See Figure 7.13)

The second way to see if a downturn of DOWJ is very near is to see the chart of TVIX, as illustrated in Figure 7.12. Examining the TVIX movement during September 2018 and SlowSTo during the same period is very instructive. While DOWJ was ascending steadily, descending speed of TVIX slowed down significantly, and SlowSTO ascended. This was a divergence of SlowSTO suggesting that DOWJ would change its direction of movement.

Figure 7.12 Chart of TVIX

Figure 7.13 Chart of DOWJ (Will DOWJ fall down soon?)

Figure 7.12 and 7.13 were updated on 6 March 2019 in Figure 7.14 and 7.15, respectively.

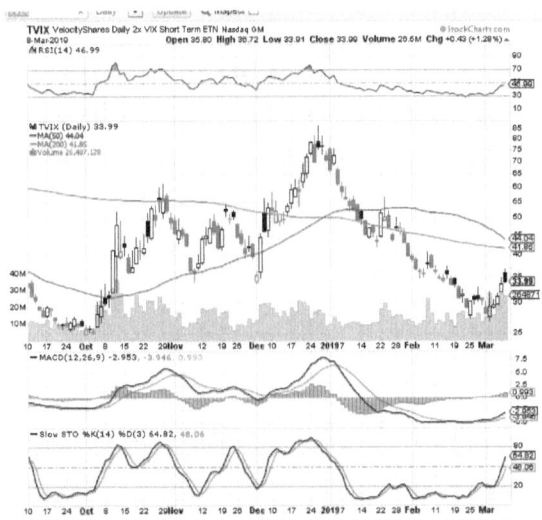

Figure 7.14 TVIX for 10 September 2018 through 8 March 2019

Figure 7.15   DOWJ for 17 September 2018 through 8 March 2019

Both Figure 7.14 and 7.15 indicate that the stock market may be in the descending mode starting about 25 February 2019. There is a chance that the DOWJ would decline with a faster speed. If the whole market fall down significantly, there can be a lucrative opportunities by buying TVIX or bear technology funds, but as of 6 March 2019, investors should wait for a few more days, or until the speed of falling will become faster.

When the direction of the market is changing, seeing the price chart of TNA may be instructive because if TNA is a fund of small stocks sensitive to the market conditions. When downturn of DOWJ started in October 2018, TNA's downturn already started one month earlier. Figure 7.16 is the price chart of TNA. Obviously the TNA started going down clearly before October 2019. We also check TZA as shown in Figure 7.17, where we see that TZA started moving upward before October. See also RSI of TZA, which was ascending during September 2019.

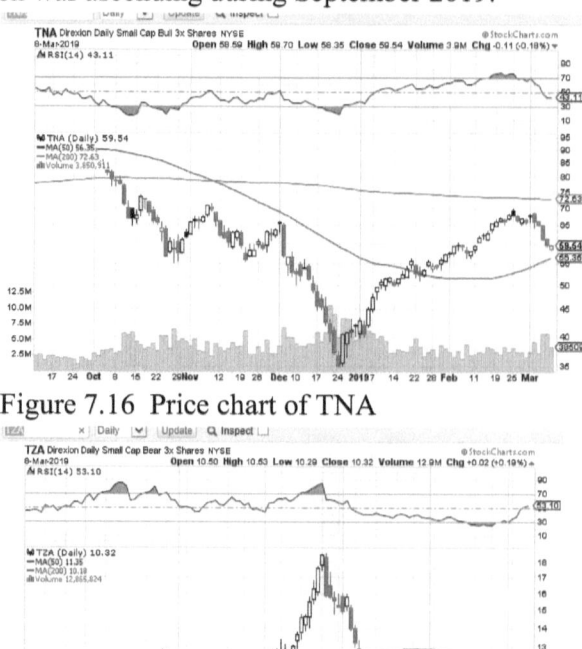

Figure 7.16 Price chart of TNA

Figure 7.16 Price chart of TZA

Another fund named SQQQ is a bear ETF and its price movements are similar to those of TVIX as shown in Figure 7.16. The reader might compare it to Figure 7.14 of TVIX. Time to buy is when DOJW starts falling down into a deep bottom.

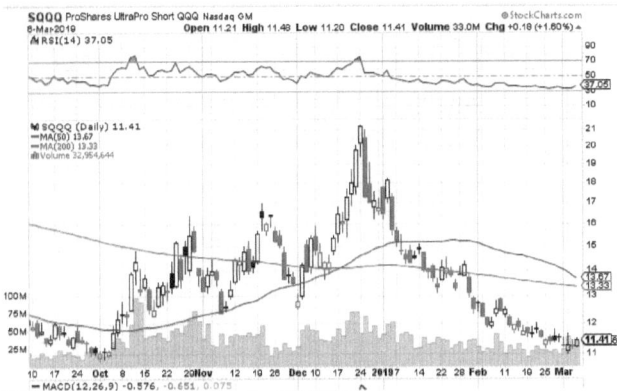
Figure 7.16 Price chart of SQQQ

The transportation ETFs are very sensitive to downturn of the stock market. Figure 7.17 shows the price chart of XTN, which is a 1x transport ETF.

Figure 7.17 Graph of XTN, a transport ETF

Notice that XTN was very clearly descending during September 2018 while SP500 and DOWJ were ascending with acceleration. As another example, the peak of XTN in late February 2019 not only appeared a few days earlier than DOWJ or TNA, the speed of descending of XTN were clearer and faster than DOWJ and even TNA. The capability of early detection of downturn of the market by XTN may be better than AD Line (see Figure 5.37).

SEA is a shipping transportation ETF which is sensitive to the economy and may be used as an economic indicator. Figure 7.18 is a price chart of SEA. The price movement after 10 January 2019 is mostly flat or even declining toward the middle of March 2019, while XTN ascended until 20 February 2019.

Figure 7.17 Price chart of SEA

7.3 Making Money in Volatile Falling Market

DOWJ started descending (see Figure 7.13) on 3 Oct 2018. The very rapid decline during 9 to 10 of October 2018 was a panic. The total loss in DOWJ between 3 October 2018 and 29 October 2018 was about 1200 or 4.6%. During this period, TVIX rose more than 100% as seen in Figure 7.12. Almost all bear ETF gained significantly as well. There is no other time when this much can be earned in the stock market. However, this is not the end of the story. DOWJ oscillated during a one and half month period thereafter. Then it continuously descended from 1 December 2018 to 24 December 2018. During this period TVIX ascended from about $36 per share to $78/share, which is a 120% increase. If TVIX was held continuously from 3 October 2018 to 24 December 2018, the gain was 210%.

During the period between 1 October 2018 and 24 December 2018, there were at least two periods when TVIX descended (DOWJ ascended). During such periods of ascending DOWJ, a bull ETF such as SOXL or TECL could have been held in order to increase the gain with TVIX further.

Finding a good timing to buy and sell TVIX is not so difficult. Before TVIX starts rising, it comes to a bottom, which occurs when the market becomes the peak. As soon as a severe down trend of the market is identified, buy TVIX, and/or bear ETFs. As soon as TVIX reaches its peak which corresponds to the bottom of the market, sell it and buy TECL or some other bull technical fund such as LABU, UBOT or SOXL. By alternating holding of TVIX and a bull technical fund, the total gain could be astounding.

7.4 Opportunities after a Bottom of DOWJ

When the DOWJ reaches a steep bottom, many stocks and ETF come to their own bottoms. The bottom of DOWJ, therefore, provides opportunities to buy stocks and funds.

The arrival of the bottom on 24 December 2018 could be detected a few days earlier by watching RSI and SlowSTO of DOWJ ($INDU) and TVIX as mentioned in the prior section. Immediately after the bottom, almost all stocks and funds started rising. Therefore, a big bottom was an extremely good opportunity to buy and the safest time to buy bull funds.

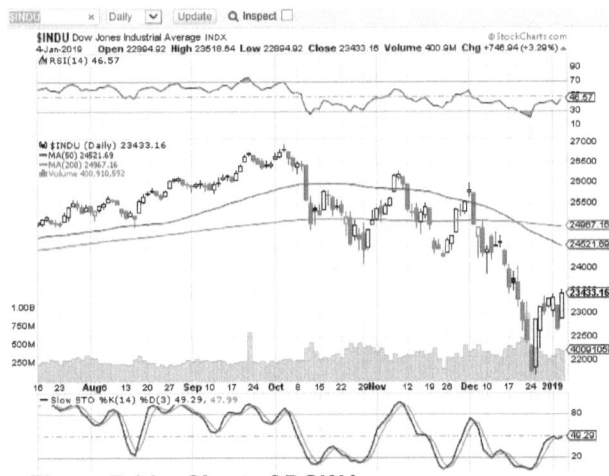

Figure 7.14 Chart of DOWJ

Figure 7.15 Chart of TECL

Figure 7.15 shows the movement of DOWJ. Its RSI and SlowSTo clearly showed that a bottom was probably happening on 24 December 2018. Actually, the large dip of the stock market on this Christmas Eve was due to thin participation of stock traders. One day after the Christmas on 26 December, there was a huge surge of DOWJ, which was due to the report of good Christmas sales. On 2 January 2019, however, DOWJ lost significantly because of the forecast of low profit of APPL due to the trade friction with China. Many funds including TECL and SOXL were affected and suffered together.

Figure 7.16 LABU (Biotech)

Interestingly LABU was little affected by AAPL as shown in Figure 7.16. The reason is that, although LABU is a technical fund, its exposure to electronics is not large. Also, RSI and SlowSTO both indicated that the price of LABU was ascending.

Figure 7.17 Price chart of WTI

Figure 7.17 shows that WTI (crude oil stock), which lost substantially (60%) since 1 October 2018, past its bottom at the same time DOWJ reached the bottom. The price recovered rapidly after 24 December 2018 and gained 40% by 5 January 2019, which is remarkable for a period of only 10 days. WTI is most sensitive to the stock market condition among other oil stocks.

A composite of price charts is shown in Figure 7.18, in which the price movements of DOWJ and nine funds are compared only for about 6 weeks including 1 December 2018 and 9 January 2019. Comparison of the price charts of various funds gives us important lessons.

The top left of Figure 7.18 is the price chart of DOWJ, which shows the bottom on 24 December 2018 and a dip on 3 January 2018. The chart of AAPL is similar except it has a huge drop with a gap on 3 January 2018, which was explained earlier. TECL and SOXL were affected by the drop of AAPL.

RUSL (Russia) reached a bottom on the same days as DOWJ, which means the Russian stock market is not free from the US stock market, although it is not affected by the dip caused by AAPL. Next, LABU, UWT, WTI, TNA and BRZU reached a bottom on the same day as DOWJ, but they were little affected by AAPL's dip except that TNA is a little affected by AAPL.

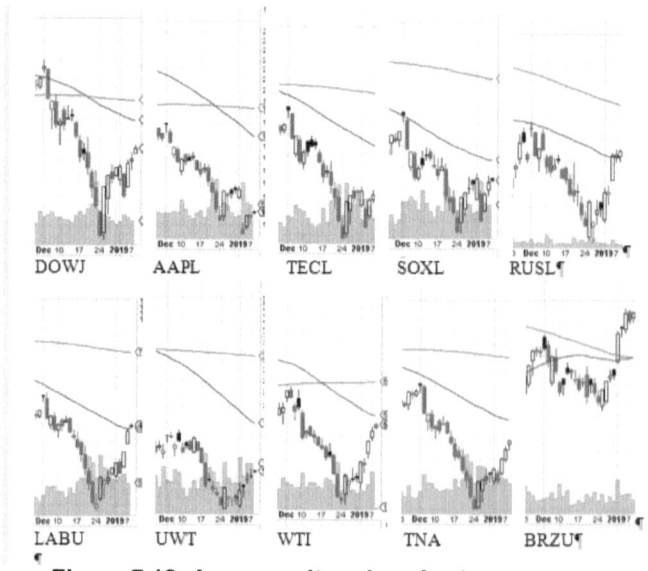

Figure 7.18 A composite price chart

7.5 How DOWJ and Gold/Gold stocks are related

We study here how DOWJ and Gold/Gold stocks are related, by comparing DOWJ and JNUG, the latter of which is a representative gold mining ETF.

In Figure 7.19, the price charts of JNUG (representing the gold mining ETFs) and DOWJ during late July 2018 through 7 January 2019 are included. As marked by black hand-written lines, there are at least 4 periods that the price movements of JNUG were in the opposite directions of DOWJ. Opposite movements are not perfect, but obvious in Figure 7.19 for the autumn of 2018. Earlier in Figure 6.48, we saw that gold price moved to the opposite directions of DOWJ in every severe decline. Figure 7.19 (18 August to 18 December 2018) demonstrates that the opposite relation between JNUG and DOWJ exists in much smaller scale of downturn of DOWJ.

Figure 7.19 Comparison between price charts of JNUG and DOWJ

However, sometimes JNUG and other gold ETFs move in tandem with DOWJ so caution is necessary.

8 Review of Stocks and Funds

This chapter is not to be read in sequence, but rather a collection of supplemental information about the stocks and funds.

The following funds have been mentioned as favorable targets of our investment:

> JNUG/JDST, NUGT/DUST
>
> TECL/TECS, SOXL/SOXS, LABU/LABD, UBOT
>
> TNA/TNZ
>
> UWT/DWT, UCO/SCO, USOU/USOD, WTI
>
> /TVIX

Here UBOT and WTI have no bear counterpart while TVIX has no bull counterpart. If you observe the price movements of above funds, you will be able to find one or two that satisfy our criteria to buy. By selling what you bought at a 20% to 30% profit, your monthly goal will be achieved.

However, it is a good practice to search more stock and funds to find further opportunities. To make survey over many stocks and funds, it is recommended to get an iPhone or iPod and save stock or fund symbols in the stock's app. With this method, scanning a large number of ticker symbols takes only a few minutes. The only disadvantage of using iPhone or iPod is that no price indicators such as RSI, MACD and SlowSTO are available. This is not a big disadvantage though, because after selecting a few stocks or fund you can open stockprices.com and study the indicators in detail.

In the remainder of this chapter, most price charts are printed on the weekly basis (one candle per week) unless otherwise stated. This is because weekly plots provide longer views and different perspectives compared to the daily plots shown in the prior chapters.

The readers are suggested to look each chart and examine how the decisions of buy and sell could be made by looking at the peaks and bottoms of the three price indicators.

DOWJ (the first figure below is a weekly chart, the second is daily)
DOWJ index is given next in both weekly and daily basis so the readers can use them to compare to other charts in the remainder of this chapter. DOWJ descended severely between October 3 and December 24, 2018. Many other stocks and funds descended together. Uninformed investors suffered losses during this period, but knowledgeable investors earned profits tremendously. The word "crisis is opportunity" applies to the stock market. The opportunities in downturns of stock market and what to do are explained in many places in this book.

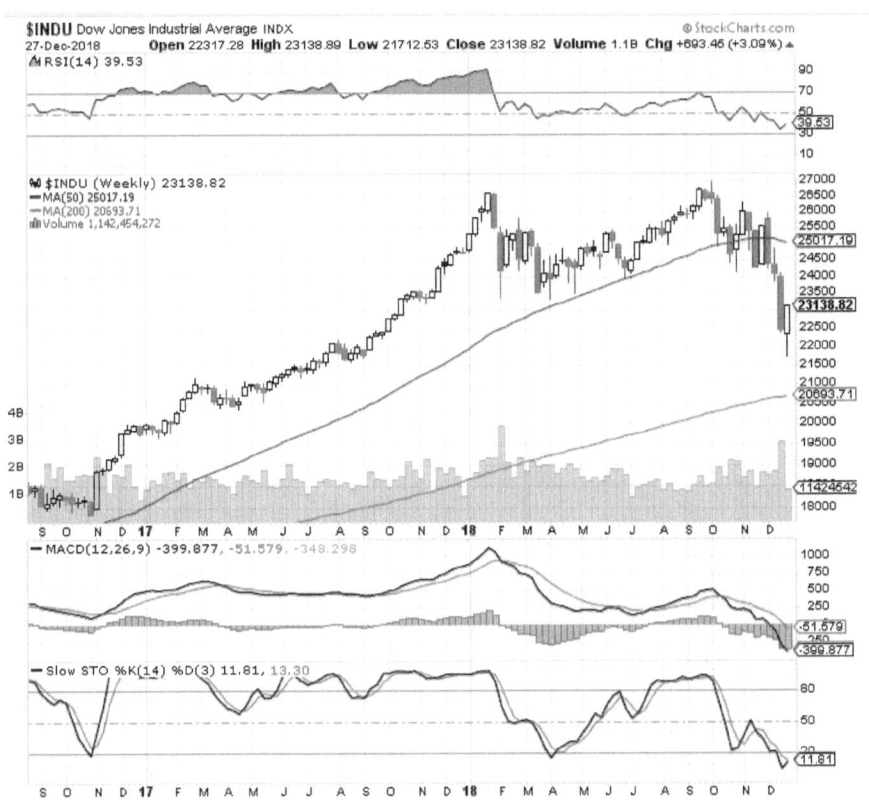

TNA small cap bull 3x ETF

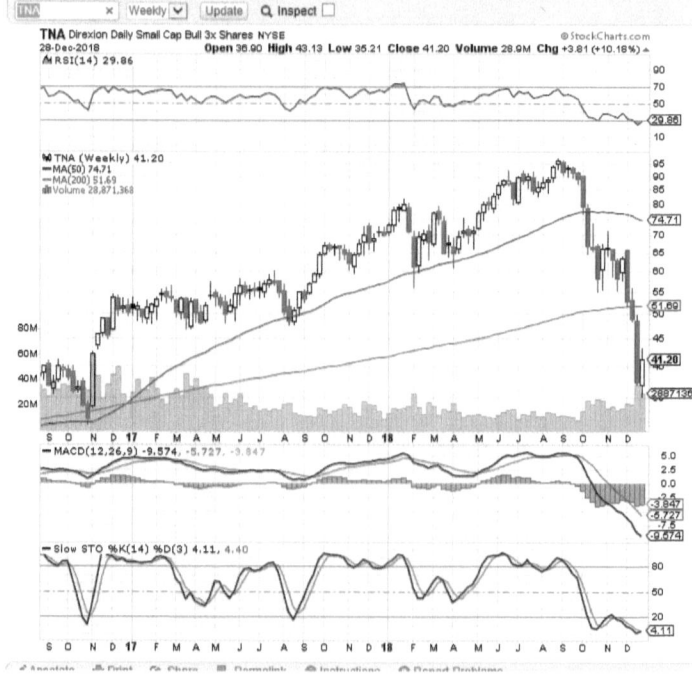

TNA is a small cap bull 3x fund. TNA Lost 63% between 1 September and 24 December 2018. The downturn of this fund started one month earlier than DOWJ. In fact, TNA started descending on 1 September 2018, while DOWJ was still ascending rapidly. Between November 2017 and October 2018, there are three major periods when SlowSTO continued to be above 80. We learn in hind sight that, when the price is in a strong ascending mode, the times SlowSTO entered the level of 80 were not good timing to sell funds because the price of funds and stocks rise significantly from that point.

Small cap funds starts downturn earlier than DOWJ or SP500. Therefore, we should check small cap funds when DOWJ or SP500 is strongly ascending.

TZA small cap bear 3x ETF

TZA is a bear counterpart of TNA. The share price gained 120% from 1 September 2018 to 24 December 2018.

GDX VanEck Gold Miner ETF

GDX is a 1x gold miner ETF, but not suitable in the way this book teaches. RSI and MACD give little information on the timing for actions. Yet, if GDX is traded in accordance with SlowSTO, a good amount of gains could be realized during the period of the above figure.

GDXJ VanEck Junior Gold Miner ETF

GDXJ is a sibling of GDX specialized in junior mining companies. JGDX tends to move faster than GDX.

JNUG Direcxion Daily Jr Gold Bull 3x ETF

JNUG is similar to GDXJ but specialized in junior gold mining companies. Its price movements are significantly larger because it is a 3x bull fund.

    The timings of buy and sell were well rendered by SlowSTO until July 2018. Trading after 1 July to the end of the year was very difficult as was explained in more details in Section 6.3. However, this problems could have been overcome by the awareness that the gold market was in a severe downtrend.

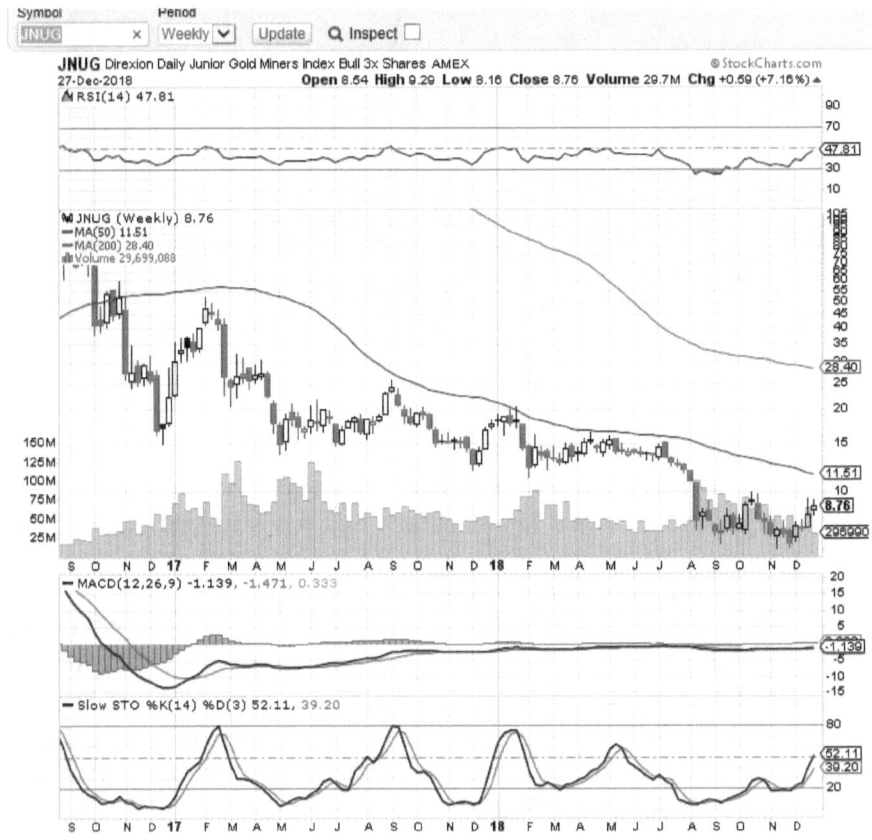

JDST Direxion Daily Jr Gold bear 3x ETF

JDST is a 3x bear junior gold mining ETF. Finding a bottom of JDST is easier than finding a bottom of JNUG. When JNUG loses a large amount value, JDST earns a huge gain. RSI and MACD do not help find the peaks and bottoms, but trading decision can be helped well by SlowSTO and by watching the shapes of candles near peaks and bottoms (see Section 5.14).

The reader may notice that, in comparison between the charts of JNUG and JDST, the price movements of JDST is not quite a reverse of JNUG. In fact while the JNUG declined during the entire period in the graph, JDST did not go up inversely. The reason is in the relatively high cost of maintenance included in the price of both funds. If the two charts are compared in a limit range less than 6 months, inverse relation can be found

As the following chart shows, JDST performed very well in late 2018 when JNUG's performance was dismal.

JNUG and JDST must be included in your list of funds for trading and bought whenever a good timing is found.

NUGT   Direxion Daily Gold Miners bull 3x ETF

NUGT is sibling of JNUG, and specialized in senior gold mining companies. It is a 3x bull ETF, and can gain much if gold price move upward.
A significant surge of gold and gold funds is expected to come in a year or two as an era of inflation approaches.

DUST   Direxion Daily Gold Miners bear 3x ETF

DUST is a bear counterpart of NUGT and is a 3x bear ETF.

An inverse relation between NUGT and DUST exist if the price movements of the two funds are compared for a limited time range for less than 6 months. However, if compared in the whole time range of the charts, both are losing the value. The reason is due to the cost of maintaining the funds included in the prices, which is the same as explained for JNUG and JDST.

ABX Barrick Gold Corporation, stock (left chart weekly, right daily)

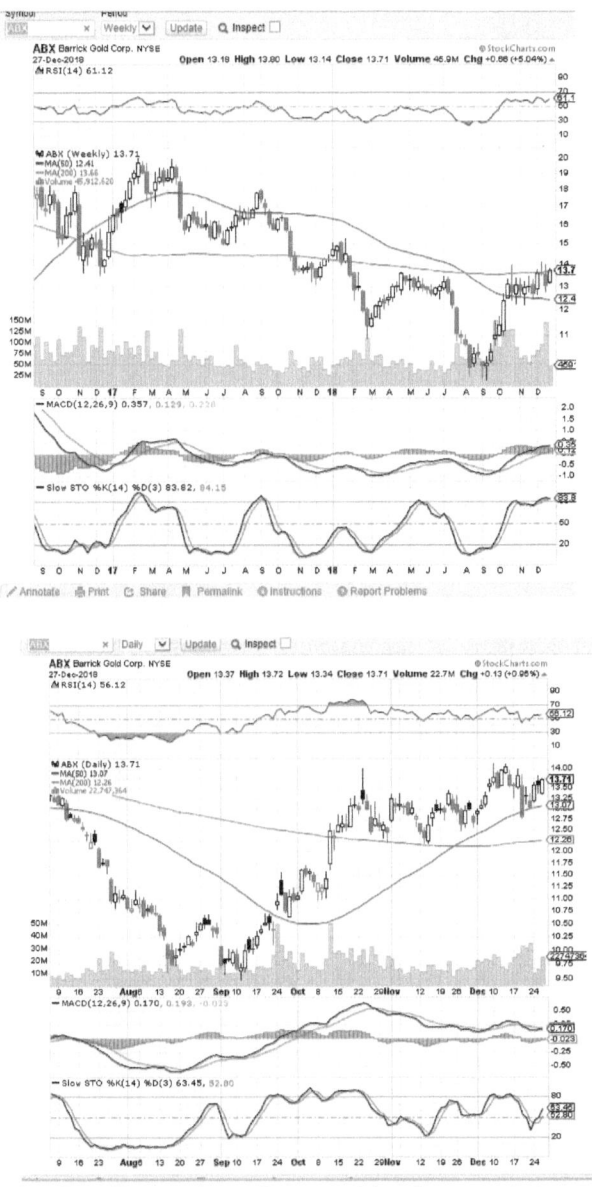

The first figure above is a weekly chart, and the second figure is a daily chart. Unlike DGX, JNUG and NUGT, ABX ascended starting in the beginning of September 2018 until November 2018.

NEM Newmont Gold Mining Company, stock

NEM is a senior gold mining company. After reaching a bottom on September 14, 2018, the stock price rebounded and ascended.

CDE Coeur Mining, Inc., stock

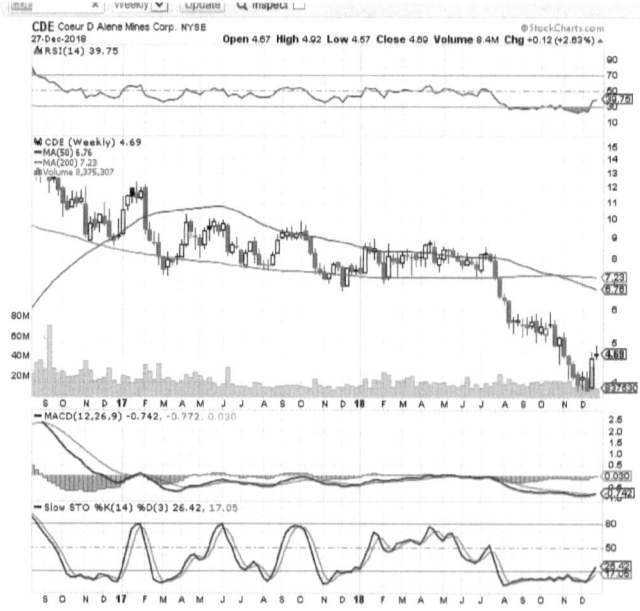

CDE is a major silver mining company. Produces gold also.

HL Hecla Mining Company, stock

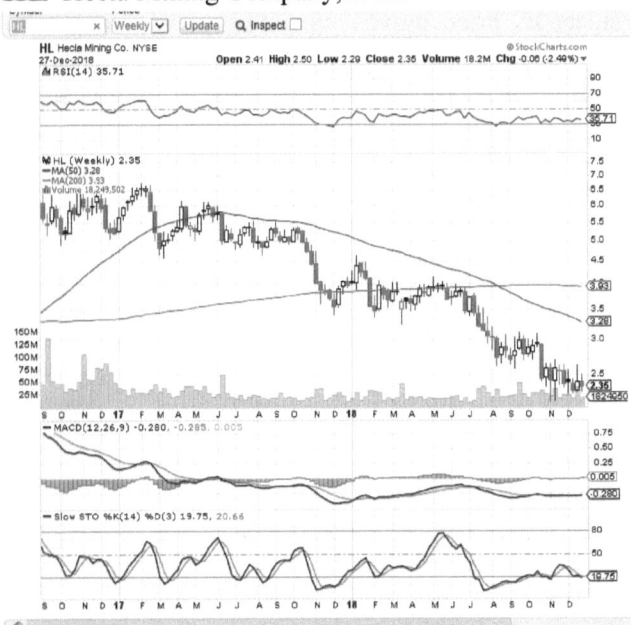

HL is a major gold mining company.

OCANF OceanaGold Corporation, stock

OCANF is a gold mining company. Its price movements are different from other gold mining companies. Its price moved up while other gold mining companies moved down in the later half of 2018. Particularly, it ascended significantly in late December 2018. Watch long wicks of the candles neat and at peaks and bottoms.

ALIAF Alacer Gold Corp, stock. The first figure below is weekly, the second is daily.

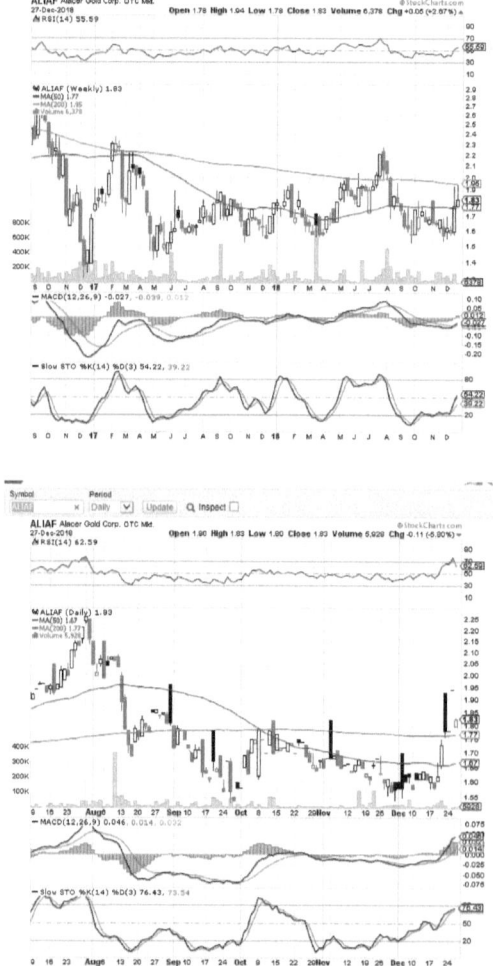

Alacer Gold Corp is a gold mining company. Its price movement has been different from other gold mining companies and attracted attention of investors. Notice very long bear candles that appear occasionally.

USLV Velocity Shares 3x bull silver mining ETN
The first figure below is weekly, the second is daily.

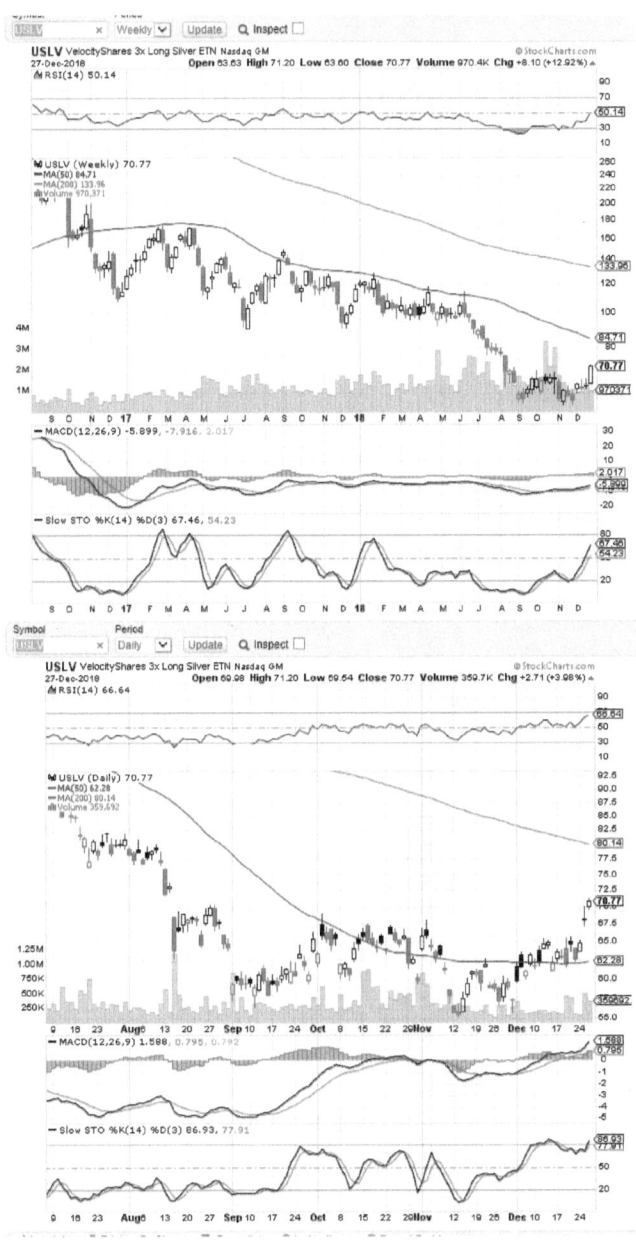

USLA is a silver mining 3x ETN. When the price movement of silver mining is positive, earning of this ETN is very attractive. Until the end of November 2018, USLV had been descending, but the price rebound was seen toward the end of 2018.

DSLV Velocity Shares 3x bear silver mining ETN

DSLV is a bear counterpart of USLV. In combination with USLV, annual gain of factor 2 could be achieved in 2018.

NG Nova Gold Resources, stock

NG is a gold mining company. The amplitudes of oscillations are relatively large. Peaks and bottoms are well rendered by SlowSTO.

AG   First Magestic Silver Corporation, stock

AG is a silver mining company. However, for our investment method, it is no better than the USLV/DSLV combination.

PVG   Pretium Resources Inc, stock

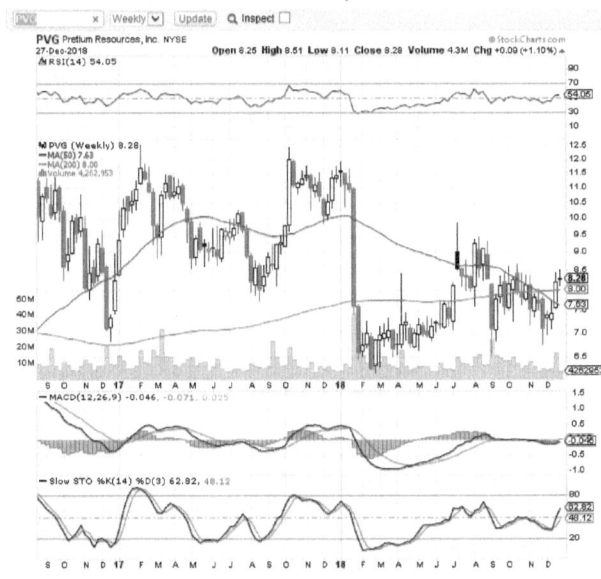

PVG is a Canadian mining company. The price wildly changed. However finding the timing for selling short is not easy because the price movements are very abrupt. For such a fund, buying at a very low and selling at a very high judging from the price chart may work better than using the price indicators, RSI, MACD and SlowSTO.

FCX Freeport McMoRan Inc, stock

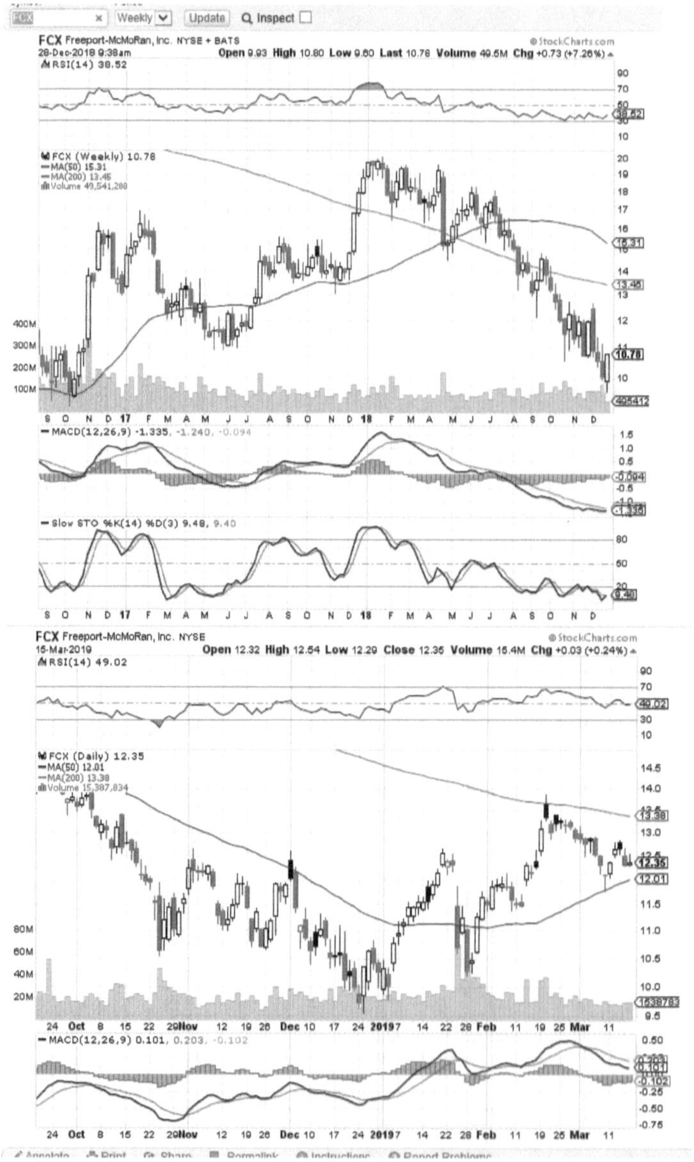

FCX is a mining company producing copper, gold and silver. Its share value increased in 2017, but lost a half of its value in 2018. In the 2.5 year chart above, substantial jumps of price are noticed in October 2016 and December 2017. After the jump in January 2018, CFX continued to descend. This stock may be sensing a few month ahead of stock market.

In the foregoing figure, a large fall in late January 2019 is noticed. The fall is extremely large compared to other stocks and funds. This stock seems to be extremely sensitive to economic predictions.

PALL Physical paradium shares ETF

PALL is an ETF tied to physical paradium. PALL has been ascending almost continuously during the past 2 and half years. Palladium is an important industrial commodity. The price of palladium is affected by the trade friction with China because China is a major producer of this metal.

GUSH Direxion gas and oil 3x bull ETF

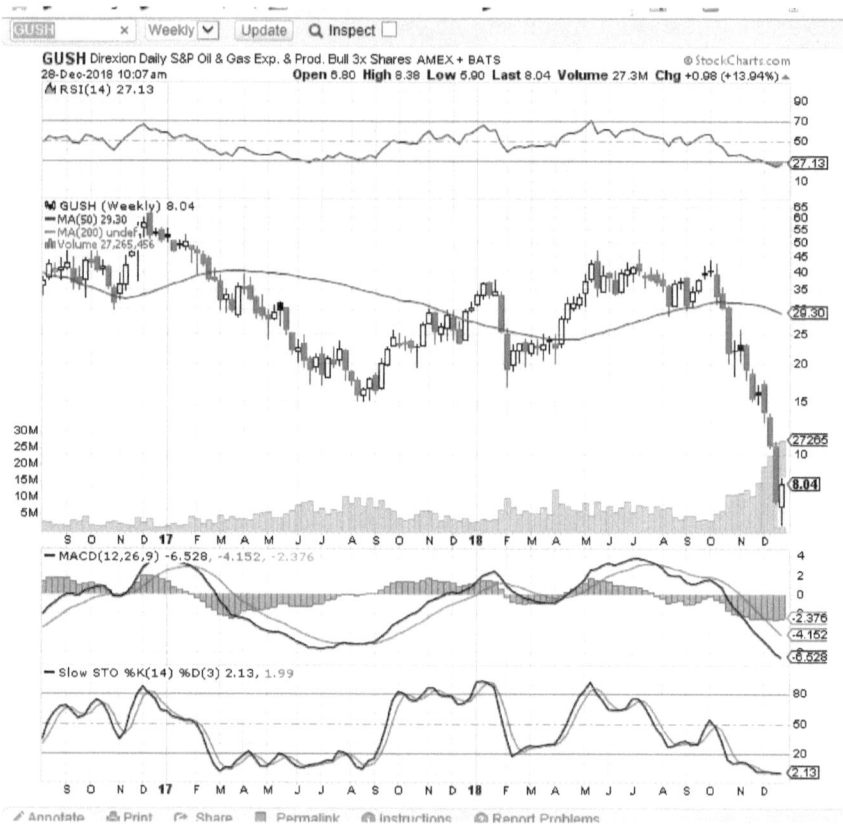

Gush is a natural gas and oil ETF. Its price movement is similar to those of UWT, USOU, GASL, ERX. It lost 80% value since the beginning of October 2018. However, both RSI and SlowSTO in the foregoing figure indicate it is oversold as of the end of December 2018, and expected to recover in 2019.

DRIP Direxion gas and oil 3x bear ETF

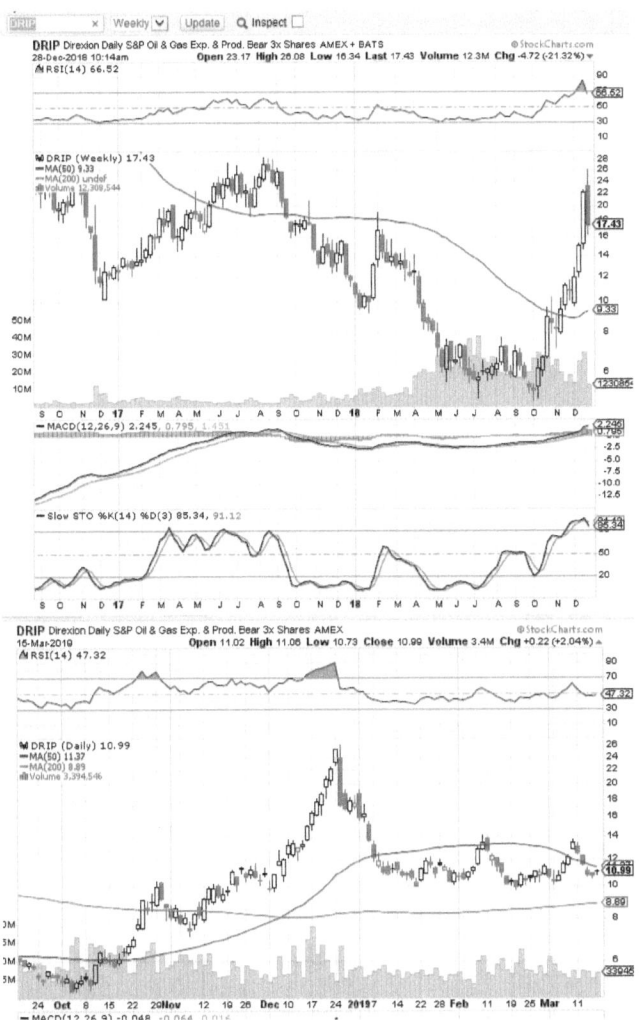

DRIP is a bear counterpart of GUSH. Its share ascended to 4.4-fold since the beginning to the end of September 2018. Both RSI and SlowSTO show that at December 27 DRIP is overbought and is coming down. We cannot see how far it will come down because, at this time of writing, the crude oil is still oversupplied and oil price may still descend in 2019.

GASL   Direxion natural gas 3x bull ETF

GASL is a natural gas bul 3x ETF. Its price movement is similar to GUSH. In fact, the amount of loss between October 1, 2018 to December 24, 2018 was 80%, similar to the loss of GUSH.

UWT Velocity Shares crude oil 3x bull ETN

UWT is a crude oil 3x bull ETN and its price movement is large when the crude oil price moves. The loss form October 1 to the end of December 2018 was 82%. UWT has been ascending gradually in 2019.

DWT   crude oil 3x bear ETN

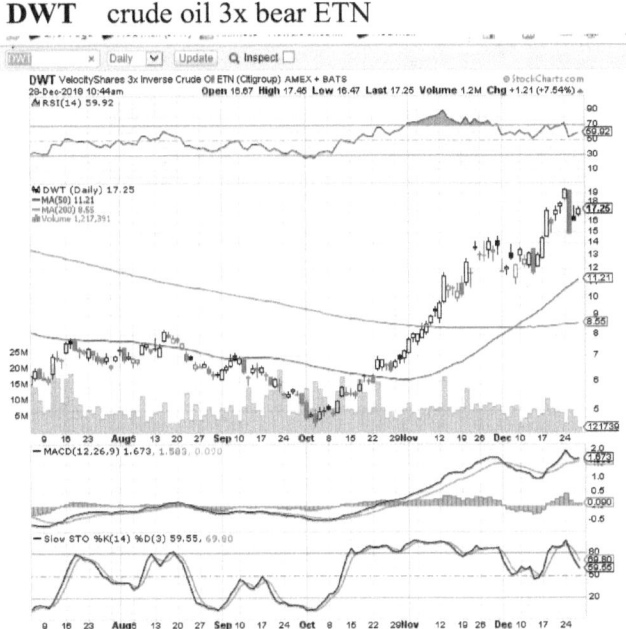

DWT is a bear counterpart of UWT. The price moved from $5 on 1 October 2018 to $19 at the peak on October 24, 2018 (280% gain). Decision of buying DWT on 1 October 2018 could have been made by the peak of RSI and the general market condition of crude oil that the price was ascending rapidly.

USOU US 3x bull oil fund (below is a daily chart)

Similarly to UWT, USOU lost 83% of the share price between 1 October and 25 December 2018. The price movement of USOU/USOD is very close to that of UWT/UWD. A very low oil price always returns to the high price before the fall. Although such a price recovery may take several months to a year, it is worth to buy oil funds when very cheap.

USOD US 3x bear oil fund (below is a daily chart)

USOD's value increased 280% between October 1 through the peak near the end of 2018. The price behavior is very similar to that of DWT.

WTI   West Texas Offshore Inc, stock (below is a daily chart)

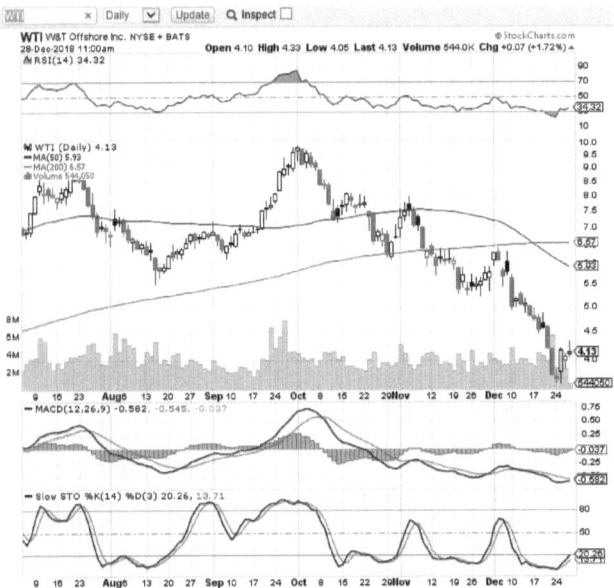

WTI is an offshore oil exploration company stock. The price movement is very high. Yet the price behavior is somewhat different than USOU or UWT, and shows a strong influence of DOWJ. WTI lost 84% between 1 October 2018 and 24 December 2018.

BP   Britich Petroream PLC, stock (below is a daily chart)

BP is a major oil company. The shape of the price movement is similar to that of WTI, although the scale of the movement is smaller. It lost 21% between 1 October 2018 and 24 December 2018.

XOM   Exxon Mobil Corporation, stock (below is a daily chart)

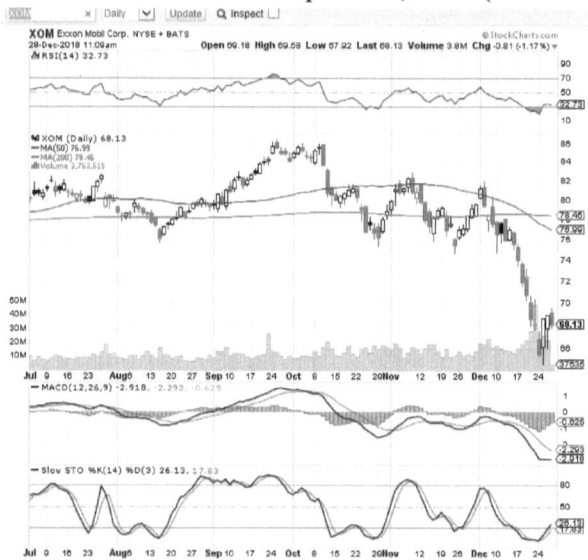

Exxon is a major oil company. Price movement is similar to that of BP.

UKOG.L   UK Oil Gas Investments PLC, stock

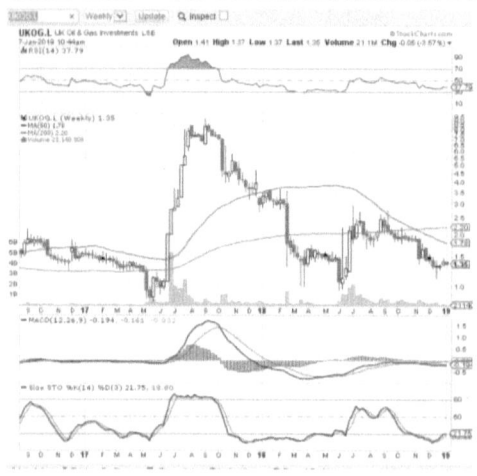

UKOG.L is an oil company of UK. Its price movement is by no means similar to other oil companies. The price movements are unpredictable.

SLCA   US Silica Holding, Inc., stock

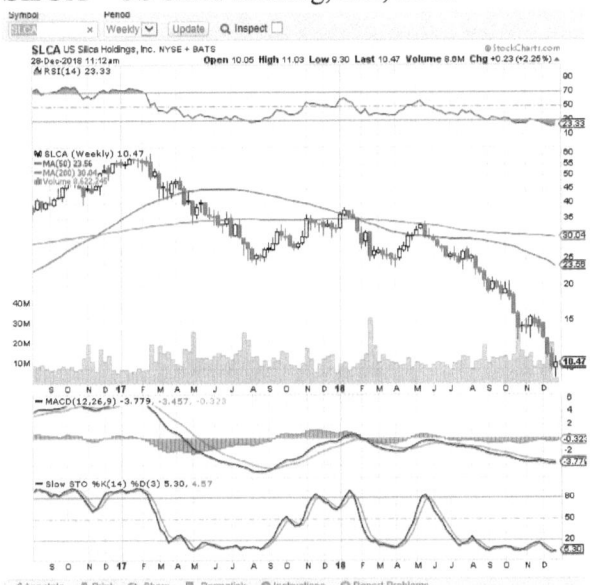

SLCA belongs to the oil industry, but its business is to sell sand. In shale oil exploration, sand mixed with a solvent in a high pressure is injected to the shale oil mine. Its share price reached a peak at the beginning of 2017, but since then the share price has been descending. Although not shown here, the price of SLCA has been recovering in 2019.

NFX   Newfield Exploration Company, stock

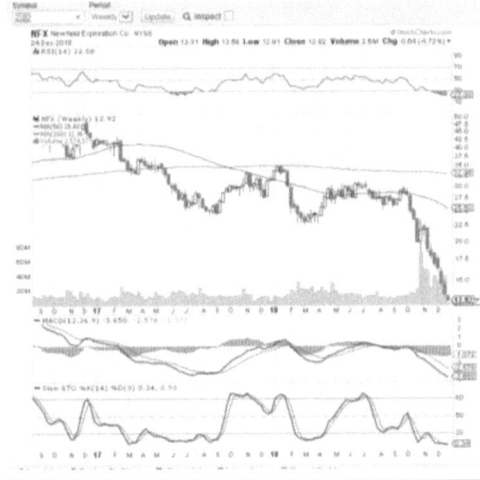

NFX is an oil exploration company. The behavior of the share price is similar to that of SLCA. Newfield merged with Encanada as of 13 February 2019.

ERX   Direxion Energy bull 3x ETF

ERX is an energy ETF. Its price movement is similar to that of BP and XOM. However, because it is a 3X bull ETF, the magnitude of price movements is far greater than BP or XOM. By 23 December 2018, it lost 63% of the value since 1 October 2018.

ERY   Direxion Energy bear 3x ETF

Bear counterpart of ERX, and its price movements are opposite to ERX. Between October 10 and December 24, its value became 180% higher. By switching between ERX and ERY, a high earning can be achieved.

FAS   Direxion Financial bull 3x ETF

FAS is a financial 3x bull ETF. FAS lost 50% from early October to 24 December 2018. Notice that MACD renders the trends of price movements well.

FAZ   Direxion Financial bear 3x ETF

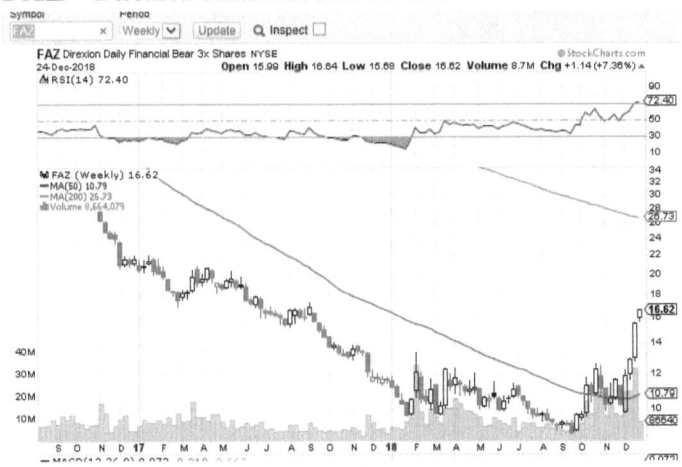

FAZ is counterpart of FAS and a bear 3x ETF. A combination of FAS and FAZ makes a powerful money making system. The ascending movement during 3 months toward the end of 2018 made the share price nearly 100% increase.

BAC Bank of America Corporation, stock

BAC issues BankAmerica Card and is a well known bank. The magnitude of price movement is relatively small.

HAL Halliburton Company, stock

HAL's business includes oil exploration, transportation and manufacturing. By buying at a bottom and selling short at a peak, this company provides good investment platform by itself. Short selling at the peak of March 2018 and buying back at the end of the year would have made the value of investment doubled. SlowSTO indicates the timings well.

X United Steel Corporation, stock

X is the largest steel company in US. Price oscillates with long wave lengths. One cycle of ascending and descending produced about 100% gains.

AEP   American Electric Power Company, stock

AEP is an electric utility company. Its stock price moves due to the economic conditions, weather and crude oil price. The stock price ascended after October 1, 2018, when DOWJ started to decline. This is because as oil price came down the cost of electric generation came down. The magnitude of stock price movements is not great enough to produce an annual gain of 100%.

BRZU   Direxion bull 3x Brazil fund

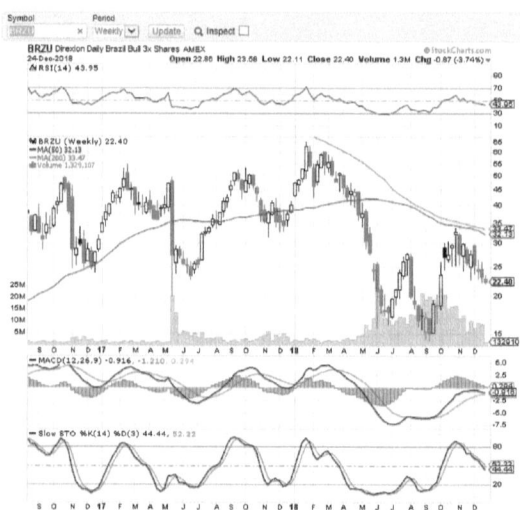

BRZU is an ETF of Brazil investment. The price of BRZU changes wildly, but independent from DOWJ. It does not have a bear counterpart. BRZU may be bought at a bottom and sold at the next peak. At its peak, this ETF may be sold short and bought back at the next bottom. Peaks and bottoms are well rendered by SlowSTO. This ETF is suitable to our method of investment.

LBJ   Direxion Latin America 3x bull

LBJ is an ETF of the investments to Latin America. Its price movement is very similar to that of BRZU. The saw tooth-like movements of the share price make it attractive to our investment methods. The amplitude of oscillation is high. There is no bear counter part.

YINN   Direxion China 3x bull ETF

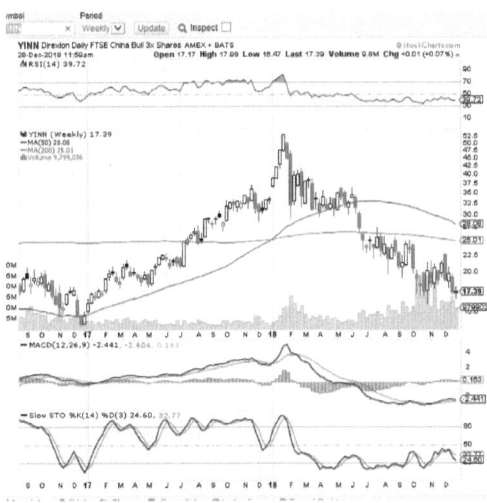

The price increase during 2017 was good, but most of the gains in 2017 was given up through the entire 2018. Future of YINN is uncertain due to the economic friction between China and US. It is interesting fund because Chinese stock market is often artificially maneuvered by the government.

RUSL   Russia bull 3x ETF

RUSL is an ETF investing in Russia. The share price oscillates wildly. Russian econmy is largely dependent on its export of crude oil, but future of Russian economy is uncertain.

RUSS Russia bear 3x ETF

RUSS is a bear counterpart of RUSL.

INDL Direxion India bull 3xETF

Price of INDL ascended well in 2017, but suffered chaotic descending in 2018. Because it does not have a bear counterpart, selling short is necessary for INDL to be a vehicle of our investment. The behavior of SlowSTO during February 2017 to October 2017 is interesting, While the price kept rising, SlowSTO was descending with some oscillation. The price movement of INDL was similar to DOWJ in 2018. In 2019, INDL is ascending at a much higher speed than DOWJ.

MEXX   Direxion Mexico bull 3x ETF

MEXX is a bull 3x ETF investing in Mexico. MEXX had a big fall in June 2018, although recovery from the bottom was fast.

AAPL   Apple Inc, stock

AAPL is one of the high quality stocks. It kept ascending since the beginning of 2017 until 3 October 2018. After then it went through an almost continuous decline of the share price until 3 January 2019. On 3 January 2019, it had a shockingly large dip. For a long term investing, it is considered to be a good stock, and the low price in early January 2019 was a good time to buy for accumulation for a long term investment. In a long term, AAPL is expected to excel other companies.

TECL Direxion Technology bull 3x ETF

TECL is a technology bull 3x ETF. Its price movement is similar to that of AAPL. If used in combination with TECS mentioned next, annual rate of yield will easily exceed our target.

TECS Direxion Technology bear 3x ETF
(The first figure below is a weekly plot, and the second figure is daily).

TECS is the bear counterpart of TECL. From October 1, 2018 to October 24, 2018, the price nearly doubled, but it came down significantly on December 26, 2018. In combination with TECL, annual yield rate will reach 200%. Peaks and bottoms are well indicated by SlowSTO. As mentioned earlier in this book, TECL comes down fast when DOWJ descends, and goes up fast when the market recovers.

UBOT Direxion Robotic Artificial Intelligence 3x bull ETF

UBOT is an ETF of robotics and artificial intelligence. It lost 67% between 1 October 2018 and 24 December 2018, but showed a good recovery in January 2019.

LABU Direxion Biotech 3x bull ETF

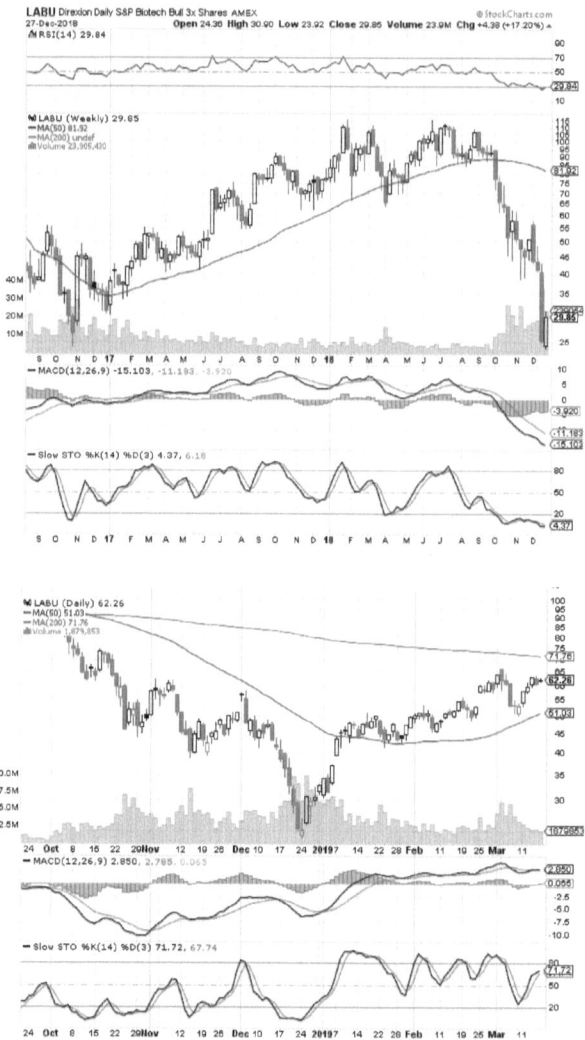

LABU is a biotech 3x bull ETF, and belongs to the technology group. Its price ascended since 2016 to the end of September 2018. During the three months period of October through December 2018, the loss of its value was 77%. LABU is, however, bouncing back upward since 26 December 2018, its recovery was very fast. This is one of the best ETF to own when DOWJ recovers from a severe bottom.

LABD   Direxion Biotech 3x bear ETF

LABD is the bear counterpart of LABU. While LABU lost significantly during the 4 months in late 2018, the value of LABD increased from $21/share to $61/share, or equivalently 190% increase. LABD is one of the best funds to own when the market is caught in a severe downturn.

DZK   Direxion Developing Market 3x bull ETF

DZK is a 3x bull ETF for investments in developing countries. In 2017, DZK ascended significaantly, but the opposite happended in 2018 with a lost of 60%. The price movement in the foregoing figure gives us a lesson, that is, if the share price is ascending but the speed of rising starts accelerated, it is the time to caution and the investors must be ready to sell. A similar phenomenon was seen in DOWJ just before DOWJ started decending in October 2018.

DPK   Direxion Developing Market bear 3x ETF

DPK is a developing market 3x bear ETF, and the bear counterpart of DZK. The share price increased 1.6-fold from October 1 to December 24. If bought in late January 2018 and sold on 24 December 2018, the gain was 100%.

NKE   NIKE Inc., stock

NKE (Nike) is a company growing fast. The share price increased almost linearly between the autumn of 2017 to September 2018, but after then the price dropped 20%. The period of descending gives us chances to selling short, and then gives us chance to buy back at the bottom.

WMT   Walmart Inc, stock

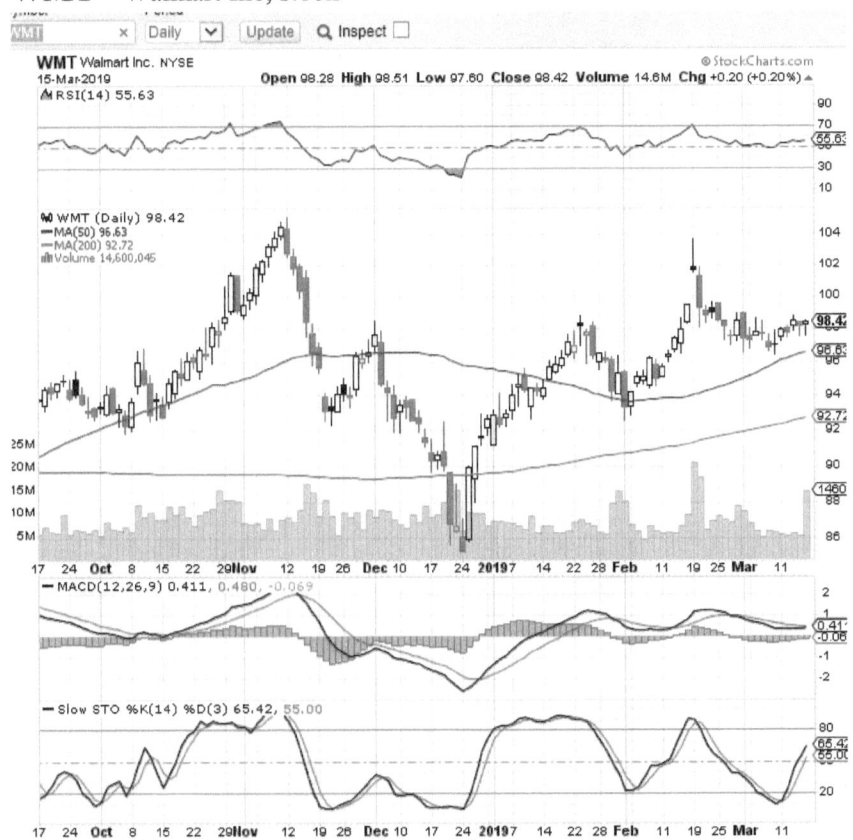

WMT is one of rapidly growing companies. It is currently challenged by Amazon, but it is developing its internet selling capabilities, and expected to compete favorably with Amazon. The movement of the prices is remarkably different from that of DOWJ. DOWJ descended significantly during the month of October 2018, but WMT ascended. WMT is good to buy when it comes to a bottom.

Notice that the candles at peaks have long wicks, which nake it easy to find the day of price reversal.

SBUX   Starbucks, stock

SBUX is a good company. Its stock price plummeted significantly in June 2018 after a trouble with an African American visitor. However, the stock not only recovered quickly, but ascended during the month of October and November 2018.

AMZN Amazon, stock

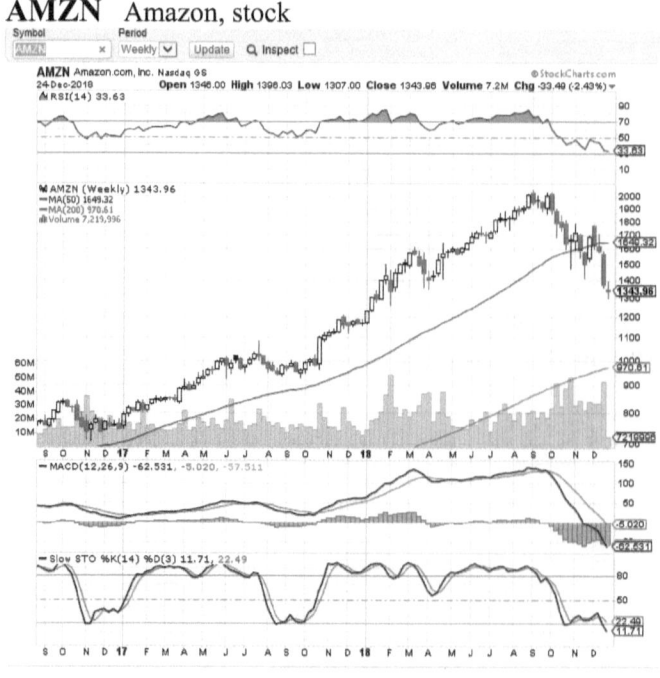

Amazon has been one of the best companies. Its stock price ascended almost linearly from November 2016 to the end of September 2018. Since then it descended significantly, but its history tells that the bottom like the end of December 2018 was a chance to buy.

SOXL   Direxion Semiconductor 3x bull ETF

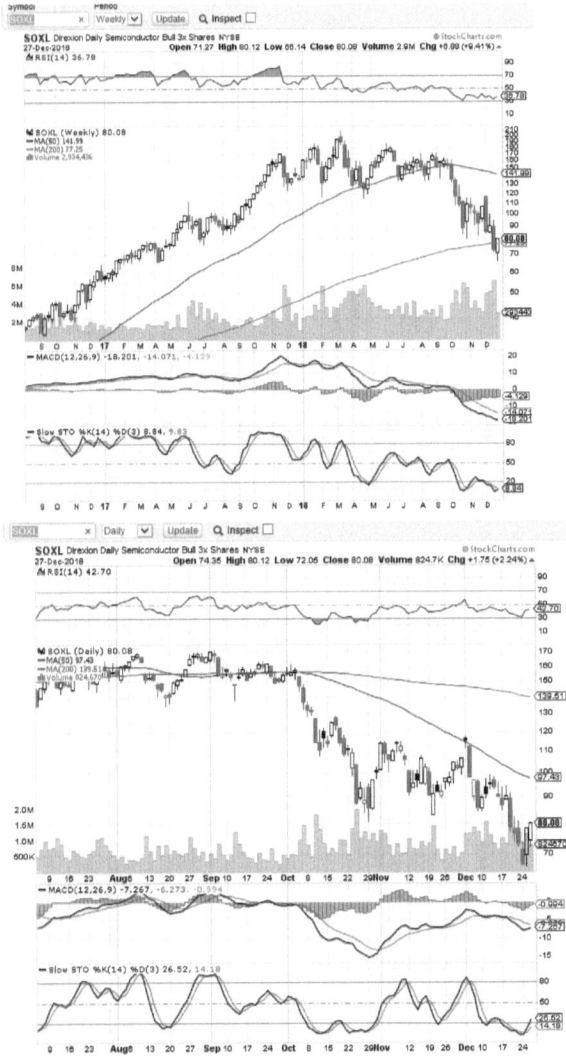

SOXL is a semiconductor 3x bull ETF. It had a tremendous advance in its value until the end of 2017. It started large oscillations in 2018, and entered a downturn starting the beginning of September 2018. By the end of 2018, SOXL lost its 61% value of October 1, 2018. However, SOXL is oversold at the end of December 2018 and the recovery of the price will be fast. SOXL is a suitable fund to our methods.

SOXS Direxion Semiconductor bear 3X ETF (below is a daily chart)

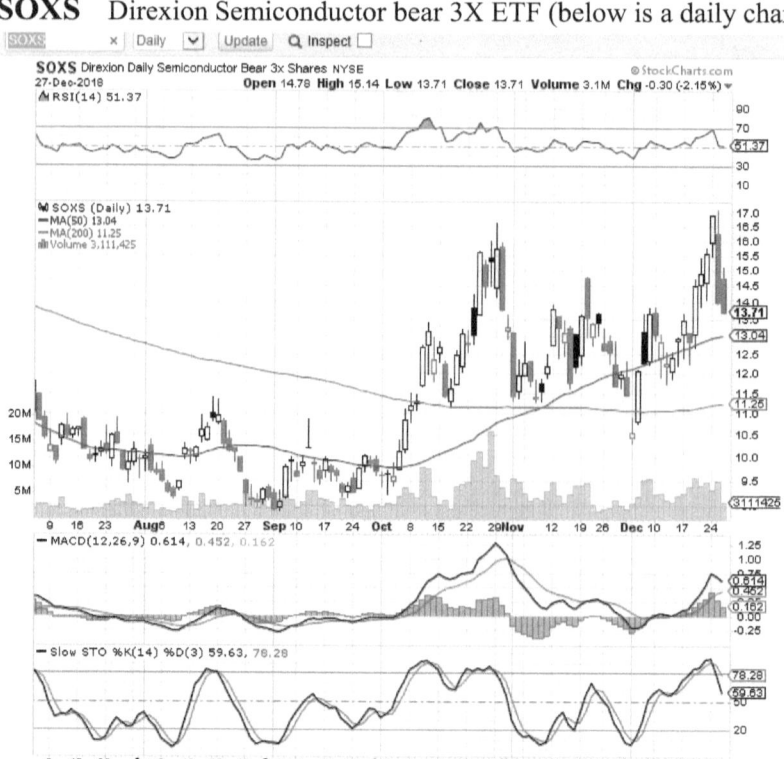

SOXS is the bear counterpart of SOXL. During the three months from October to the end of December 2018, its value gained 79%. This a good fund to buy in downturn of the stock market.

WDC Western Digital, stock

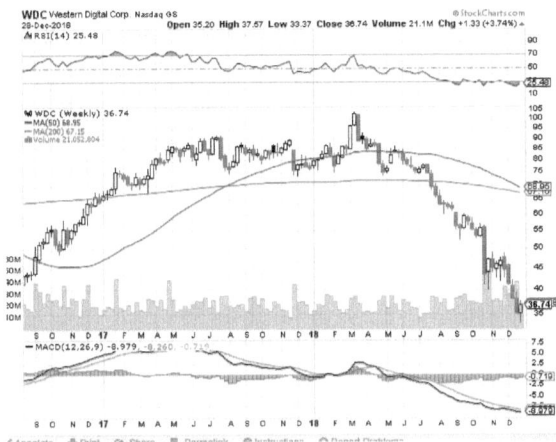

WDC is a computer disk maker, but is suffering from recent poor sales of PC. The price movement is similar to that of SOXL, but the speed of the price descending in 2018 was faster than that of SPXL. We will watch to see if the price movement would turn to ascending as DOWJ recovers in 2019.

AMX American Movil, stock

AMX is a Mexican telephone company. AMX is affected by DOWJ but still shows some independence from DOWJ. Its bottoms are well rendered by SlowSTO.

FB FaceBook, stock

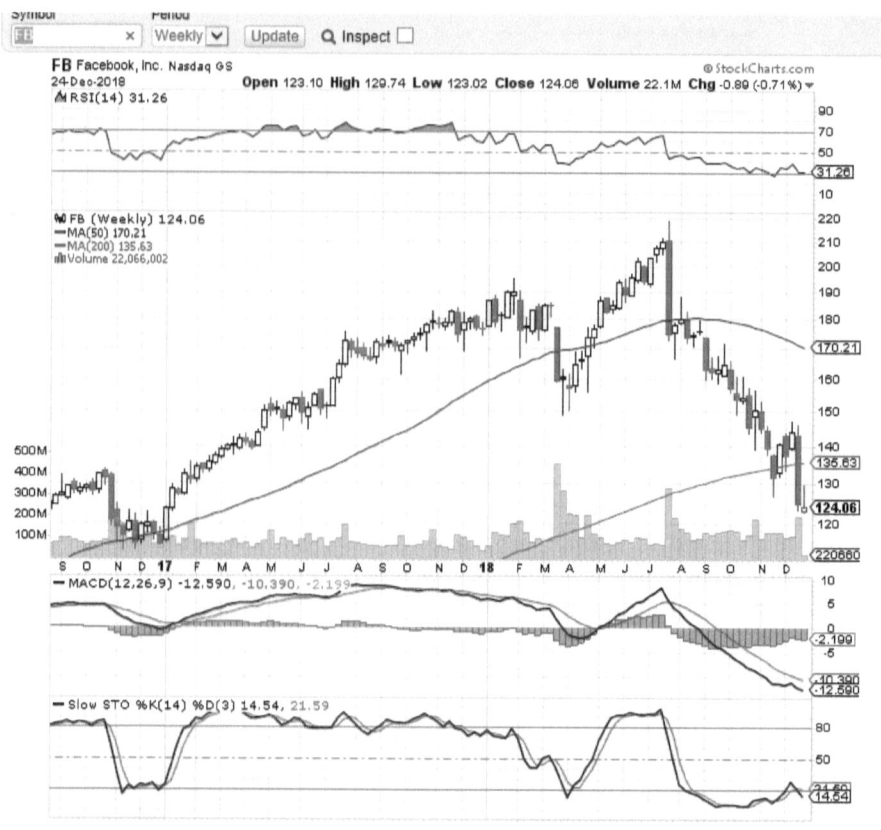

FB has been a rapidly growing company. In March 2018, however, its stock price plummeted about 30% due to privacy and hacker problems. Since then, the price recovered and exceeded the previous peak but the price dropped fast in late July 2018.

9 Rules of What To Do Now

[1] Open an online brokerage account such as Fidelity or Ameritrade, and transfer some money from your bank account to the brokerage account. Set your account so trading becomes possible with some margin. Between Fidelity and Ameritrade, the former is easier to make trades because of more user-friendly design of the forms to work with when buying and selling stocks or funds.

[2] Make sure you understand how to use RSI, MACD, and SlowSTO.

[3] The price charts in this book will be outdated by the time you read this book, although the fundamental principle of trading will remain unchanged. It is suggested for the reader to update the price charts and find out the current situation. Make sure SlowSTO is added to each price chart.

[4] Check the general market condition everyday by opening the price chart of $INDU(DOWJ), XTN, TNA, TVIX, JNUG, UWT, SOXL plus whatever the funds you are interested in. Examine and record the price, RSI, MACD and SlowSTO of each.

[5] Look at the candle shape at peaks and bottom in the price chart and review what was explained in Section 5.14.

[6] Determine if the price of stock or fund is ascending or descending. If the price is rising in acceleration, estimate from the chart how soon the next peak will arrive. Likewise if the price is descending, estimate from the chart how soon the next bottom will arrive.

[7] Buy a 2x or 3x bull fund (ETF or ETN) only when the price is at a bottom price, or as close to the bottom price as possible. The day of bottom price should be found by looking at the shape of the candle (Section 5.14) with assistance of price indicators, RSI, MACD and SlowSTO. For bottom day, RSI may not be necessarily below 30. Likewise SlowSTO may not be below 20. The best time to buy is before closing of the bottom day.

[8] Sell a 2x or 3x bull fund (ETF or ETN) only when the price is at a peak price, or as close to the top price as possible. The day of peak price should be found by looking at the shape of the candle (Section 5.14) with assistance of price indicators, RSI, MACD and SlowSTO. For a top day, RSI may not be necessarily above 70. Likewise SlowSTO may not be above 80. The best time to sell is before closing of the peak day.

[9] When you are not certain, do not buy. If you have bought a fund, but you become uncertain about where the price will go further, get out by selling the fund. As you get more experienced in trading, your skill to judge the situation will increase. Do not get into love with the fund you bought. It will become your enemy and hazard if it starts losing the value.

[10] After you bought a fund, the price ascending may not be straight but often the price goes up and down. Hold the fund you bought as long as the indicators tells the stock or the fund is in the course of ascending. If it starts making a peak with a candle with long upper wick and then coming down, be fast to sell. Also the stock market may get a sudden unexpected fall and price of many funds and stocks may be shaken. It is mostly a one-day event and tends to recover next day. Such a one-day drop happens when a bad news of one of the major companies is reported. For such an incidence, the stock price indicators do not show much movement. So keep holding.

[11] When the price starts going up, and approaches an oversold territory (RSI>70, or SlowSTO>80), be ready to sell, but don't sell immediately because the price may rise significantly from there. Sell the fund only when you are convinced that the price reached the peak with a candle with a long upper wick. Same applies to the timing of buying, that is, do not buy immediately after SlowSTO passes 20 from above because the price may still descend significantly. Buy only when the price reached the real bottom with a candle with a long lower wick, or confirmed to have reached the bottom.

[12] For a novice investor, do not use all the money you have. Always keep a half in cash until your trading makes a series of success.

www.ingramcontent.com/pod-product-compliance
Lightning Source LLC
Chambersburg PA
CBHW021412210526
45463CB00001B/328